W9-BZE-952

IN THIS SERIES . . .

TC SERIES IN **SPECIAL EDUCATION**

MAURICE H. FOURACRE, EDITOR

Guiding the
Physically Handicapped
College Student

HERBERT RUSALEM

Hunter College of the
City University of New York

BUREAU OF PUBLICATIONS

Teachers College, Columbia University
New York, 1962

Foreword

SPECIAL EDUCATION for exceptional individuals has had a spectacular growth in the past decade. This growth has been manifest in all sectors of the field; in numbers of children served, in the quality of programs on the national, state, and local levels, and in community support of educational efforts on behalf of children and adults with physical, mental, and emotional problems. A major consequence of this growth pattern has been the rising tide of severely limited children who have been accepted into and educated through our schools. In unprecedented numbers, such children are being given educational opportunities which were not available to them just a few years ago.

By assuming increased responsibility for the educational, social, and vocational development of its exceptional children, the American community has committed itself to finding solutions to a number of consequent problems. Perhaps the most pressing of these problems is that of the postschool adjustment of disabled persons. Now that the schools are providing improved educational service to exceptional children, we must turn our attention more fully to the conditions under which these children will put this education to work after they have completed the school program. This brings us into an area that is full of thorny problems, including community attitudes toward the disabled, the availability of postschool training and rehabilitation services, and the opening of new vocational opportunities for the severely disabled.

v

One of the most significant areas of growing concern to general and special educators is that of college attendance of the exceptional. The pressures of modern society are in the direction of increased college enrollments. It is expected that an ever-growing proportion of American youth will be entering American institutions of higher education. This fact will be even more true of exceptional youth. Improved special education, expanding rehabilitation services, and favorable changes in public attitudes are all contributing to stimulate exceptional children to consider college attendance as an alternative. It may be expected that this flow of severely physically disabled students toward college campuses will grow even larger in the next decade.

Many colleges and universities are unprepared for the tide of exceptional individuals who are knocking on their doors. A few have developed rich programs for disabled students, offering a variety of services to enhance and facilitate the education of students with serious physical problems. In most cases, however, special education, as a specialty, has just begun to penetrate higher education. Until now, exceptional students have been served on an individual basis without the benefit of formal policies, procedure, and methods. But this will probably change as the exceptional student becomes a familiar figure on the American campus.

It seems likely that a branch of special education will develop which will concern itself with college students. There is already some evidence that this is happening. Dr. Rusalem's book is an early attempt to explore this new specialty in special education, reflecting the current status of the field. Thus, he has been able to draw relatively little from the experimental literature and has had to rely largely on his own observations and experiences. However, it is important for the field of special education that college students be launched in a professional way. We believe that, in publishing this material, the Teachers College Series in Special Education will be contributing to this goal. At the same time, this book will have value for those who work with exceptional college students, suggesting approaches to common service problems.

During his career as a teacher of exceptional children, an administrator of a program, and a college instructor in special education, Herbert Rusalem has acquired considerable experience in the area of higher education of the physically disabled. Currently, he has responsibility for a counseling program for physically handicapped college students in a large educational institution. In addition, he has participated in numerous rehabilitation research projects, many of which have dealt with students at this level. Out of all this experience has come the conviction that, given adequate opportunities, severely disabled students may function successfully within the established standards and norms of many colleges and universities in the United States. This book suggests the nature of such opportunities and how they may be widened.

MAURICE H. FOURACRE
Head, Department of Special Education
Teachers College, Columbia University

Contents

Guiding the
Physically Handicapped
College Student

The Physically Handicapped Student on the College Campus

EACH YEAR, thousands of physically handicapped* students apply for admission to American colleges and universities. Their exact number has not been determined. A sampling of a few large institutions suggests that this special college population runs into the tens of thousands. Some have mild limitations which will have only minor influence on their college programs. Others are severely disabled, with limitations which affect many aspects of college attendance. Still others have limitations so pervasive that personnel in the institution question the desirability of enrolling them.

The trend in college attendance of physically handicapped students can be measured only by the crudest of yardsticks. Yet college administrators tend to believe that their numbers and the severity of their disabilities are on the increase. Colleges and universities are and will continue to be confronted by the need to serve individuals with a variety of disabilities. Most common among these are limitations in vision, hearing, mobility, manipulative ability, physical vigor, and endurance.

It is the purpose of the present writer to explore the ramifications of working with physically disabled persons on the college campus and to suggest procedures which may improve the quality of the educational service provided for them. In addition, an effort

* There has been a tendency in the professional literature to differentiate "handicap" from "disability." For the purposes of this book, this differentiation is not material. Hamilton's definition of "handicap" will be used here to denote both handicap and disability. This definition is: A handicap is the cumulative result of the obstacles which a physical, mental, or emotional condition interposes between the individual and his maximum functional level. [26] (Paraphrased.)

will be made to suggest the impact of such attendance on the administration, faculty, curriculum, and leisure-time activities of the institution of higher learning. Because the range of individual differences among disabled students is as extensive as among all students, and because the term "physical handicap" connotes a long continuum of degree of severity and limitations, only the broadest of generalizations can be offered. Service to the individual student must be based on a selective application of the principles set forth in this volume to his needs. This requires a comprehensive study of each physically handicapped student and preparation of an individual program within the general policies and procedures of the institution.

The term "physically handicapped" does not necessarily establish a commonality among individuals so designated. [2] A person with a relatively minor limp, another with total loss of vision, a wheel-chair patient with a degenerative disease, and a student who functions normally except for a seizure every few weeks are all classified as "physically disabled." Within each of these categories, a few similarities may be identified among students with that disability. Yet the intra-disability group differences are highly significant. For example, some persons who are legally blind are relatively self-sufficient in mobility and communication; others are not. Some hearing losses are more limiting than others. Some individuals on crutches achieve safety in mobility; others do not.

In addition to the evident differences in type and severity of disability, differences are introduced in terms of the age at onset of disability, type of home and hospital care received, the cosmetic effect of the handicap, the presence or absence of pain and discomfort, social attitudes toward the disability, and the psychological impact of the limitation on the student. From this it may be gathered that the problem of the physically disabled student is not merely that of a physical loss. Evidence in the area of psychological aspects of physical disability suggests that social perceptions and self-attitudes play major roles in determining the degree of actual handicap. [4, 15, 65] Thus, because of psychological factors, two individuals with a similar physical loss may function quite differently.

In view of the psychophysical complexity of physical disability, is it possible to state an operational definition which will have functional value for the reader? To facilitate discussion, it seems advisable to define the broad limits of the student population to be discussed in this volume. Therefore, the following definition is offered:

A physically handicapped college student is one having activity limitations ascertainable by a physician and other professional personnel which affect his functioning on the campus to such a degree that one or more special services not offered to other students and/or intensified existing services are required for his continued successful functioning, academically and/or socially.

For our purposes, students are not considered physically handicapped unless the disability interferes with successful college attendance. In this framework we are not concerned with the student who has a medically significant physical problem if that problem does not create a need for college services other than those normally available to students in general. On the other hand, some individuals who have medically ascertainable conditions of less objective significance from the physician's point of view may require special services. For example, because of emotional factors, a student with a relatively mild hearing loss may require special counseling, special tutoring, and special class placement, while another student with a profound loss may require no special services at all, as long as he wears his hearing aid.

All this introduces the concept that, from the point of view of college service, the physically disabled student is not a member of a diagnostic category and, *ipso facto,* presumed to have certain needs. [64] On the contrary, in addition to the useful guide provided by the diagnosis and the specifications of limitations, the use he is making of his residual capacities should be spelled out. Some have made successful adjustments and can function independently. Others with roughly the same condition function quite differently. In the light of the definition offered, the need for special services in the college may be determined by a medical-social team rather than by medical personnel alone. The disabled student is more than a physical condition. He is an individual who has feelings about the condition and has achieved a way of life in which he comes to terms with it in a variety of ways. These individual responses to disability are crucial to an understanding of the disabled student. A college program for this group must be built on an assessment of these psychosocial elements along with the medical facts, and adapted as the student moves through his college career.

COLLEGE ATTENDANCE AND THE PHYSICALLY HANDICAPPED STUDENT

Physically disabled students attend college for much the same reasons as other students. The patterns of motivation are individual and varied. The dominant interest may be self-realization, an affection for learning, status, parental pressure, vocational plans, the expectations for youth in a particular social class, the influence of a key person, improvement in social level, or other factors.

It is difficult to generalize about the role of college attendance in the life of the physically handicapped student. [19] In some instances, it represents an opportunity for emancipation from overprotecting parents. In others, it may be a chance to work and live with nonhandicapped persons. For still others, it may indicate the beginning of reality testing in an environment where the standards of performance are objective and unrelated to the disability.

Although group motivations defy description, the motivations of the individual student are important. Through knowing the major reasons which brought a handicapped student to college, instructors and counselors may better understand his problems and performance in the college setting. Consequently, in assessing a disabled student's readiness for college attendance, college personnel will want to know the applicant's perception of the values of a college experience for him. In this way, some evidence may be developed pertaining to the suitability of a particular institution for a particular student.

Two special factors in the education and rehabilitation of physically disabled young people may play roles influencing the decision to attend college and the goals to be achieved at college.

Vocational Rehabilitation

In every state in the United States, joint federal-state vocational rehabilitation agencies serve individuals with physical, emotional, and mental disabilities. These agencies function in a framework of state and federal legislation and offer a variety of services to eligible individuals possessing handicaps which constitute a deterrent to remunerative employment. [17] A more extended description of the contributions of these agencies to the disabled college student appears in Chapter 6. For the present, it is sufficient to note that the following services are available to college students and others who meet the criteria of eligibility and feasibility: medical and vocational diagnosis; medical treatment; prostheses, hearing aids, eyeglasses, and other aids; prevocational and vocational training, including attendance at collegiate institutions; provision of training materials, such as textbooks, recording machines, etc.; vocational counseling; placement; placement equipment, such as tools to enable an individual to start in his occupation; and follow-up and research.

A large number of vocational rehabilitation agencies become interested in disabled students while they are still in secondary school. Others begin to make contact with them at the time of entrance into college. In either event, college personnel will generally find that a large proportion of severely disabled applicants for admission are known to the state vocational rehabilitation agencies. If it is believed that the student is otherwise eligible and that he has the intellectual capacity, physical competence, and emotional readiness for higher education, the vocational rehabilitation agency may "sponsor" his college attendance. This sponsorship varies from provision of vocational counseling to significant financial contributions toward fees and maintenance expenses during the college period. [29]

With this in mind, the influence of the rehabilitation program on student motivation to attend college becomes more clear. Currently, the emphasis in the State-Federal Rehabilitation Program is on the vocational. In most cases, clients of these agencies will have had vocational counseling by rehabilitation counselors prior to the decision to enter college and the selection of an institution. A product of this counseling is a vocational plan. Generally, sponsorship is not offered to the student who wishes to pursue a college education without consideration of its impact on his vocational adjustment.

Consequently, the disabled student's thinking is likely to be influenced by vocational considerations which play an important part in his becoming a suitable candidate for vocational rehabilitation service. In addition, if the applicant is admitted to a college and attends with the approval and support of the state rehabilitation agency, follow-up interviews with agency personnel will keep the vocational values of college attendance sharply in the student's focus. As a result of this, the physically disabled group of students may be expected to perceive college in pronouncedly vocational terms. However, this probability does not necessarily exclude other parallel perceptions of the value of a college education.

Post-High School Employment Opportunities

All students face a variety of alternatives on graduation from high school. Some enter college. Others receive training at non-college institutions, secure jobs in industry, enter the armed services, or take on the duties of homemaker. For some physically disabled students, post-high school alternatives are fewer in number. For example, a severely disabled cerebral palsied youth may not be admitted to trade or technical training, or to a job in competitive industry; the armed services will be closed to him, and the homemaking role may be inappropriate.

When there are few alternatives for a severely disabled youth in the post-high school world, college attendance may be considered a logical choice. However, a number of authorities in the field of the education and rehabilitation of handicapped youth have observed that some members of this group should not attend college. [19, 35, 39] They question the academic and physical qualifications of some of these students, and believe that limited post-college employment opportunities in the professions argue against higher education for all who would make this choice. They cite cases illustrating the frustration and disappointment of severely disabled young people who, upon completing a degree program, are rejected by potential employers in their chosen fields.

In addition to the usual motivations which bring students into a college program, some disabled students are attracted to undergraduate work because of the lack of other feasible plans. Not infrequently, parents and counselors stress this factor. The parents may feel that college attendance will provide prestige, preparation for a profession, and improved personal functioning to their children. The counselor may be unable to suggest alternative plans and, in desperation, put off the "day of decision" for the four or more years required to complete the college program. The motivational patterns related to selection of college attendance are not simple. Often, the motivations which have brought the disabled student to the campus are not the ones which keep him there and prevail throughout his college career. The process of maturation, the separation from the familiar home and school environment, and the influence of academic and other college experiences may revise the student's motivational structure.

Students who came largely to satisfy parental desires may find a new meaning for their lives on campus and may follow a college career for personal enrichment, social development, and love of learning. Through awareness of the changing pattern of student motivations, college instructors and counselors may achieve a better understanding of the disabled student and may be better able to serve him.

FACTORS ACCOUNTING FOR THE INCREASING ENROLLMENT OF PHYSICALLY HANDICAPPED STUDENTS IN COLLEGES AND UNIVERSITIES

Administrators of colleges and universities believe that the number of physically handicapped students on campus is increasing. Although census figures are lacking, other evidence appears to support this position.

Growth of Special Education Facilities

During the past decade, the education of severely disabled children in regular public school classes, in special public school classes, and in special schools has had a phenomenal growth. [17] Special education services in the local community have been extended not only to increasing numbers of disabled children, but to children whose severity of disability has previously excluded them from school attendance. Among these have been children with epilepsy, cerebral palsy, muscular dystrophy, multiple sclerosis, paraplegia, multiple handicaps, and others. [37]

An important aspect of this growth has been the development of new and modified secondary education facilities for these children. Increasing numbers of homebound children all over the country have achieved high school graduation through home instruction, school-to-home telephone, and other devices. Thus, an increasingly large number of severely disabled youth have been prepared to undertake college-level study. A mounting proportion of these students are applying for admission.

Expansion of Rehabilitation Services

Stimulated by new legislation and a growing public awareness of the potentialities of comprehensive team services, rehabilitation has moved forward at an accelerated pace during the past decade. [2, 34] A number of changes in the field have given added strength to it. Among these have been:

1. The advancement of medical knowledge and skills and the emergence of the specialty of physical medicine and rehabilitation.

2. The growing body of research.

3. The emphasis on rehabilitation centers and the development of integrated service programs.

4. The stimulus given by the Office of Vocational Rehabilitation to professional training in the various disciplines that make up the rehabilitation team.

5. Effective community education efforts by public and private agencies.

6. The availability of larger sums of money for rehabilitation purposes.

7. The evolution of a community-centered concept of rehabilitation organization.

A major consequence of this increased effort in rehabilitation has been the extension of service to severely disabled individuals. A number of the handicapped groups currently being served were thought to be nonsusceptible of rehabilitation only a few short years ago. Today, services are rendered to persons with extensive losses and with multiple disabilities. Among these are the cerebral palsied, the paraplegics, the homebound, the deaf, the blind, the epileptic, the mentally retarded, and the emotionally handicapped. A proportion in each of these groups is emerging from the rehabilitation service with plans for further educational and vocational activities. In some cases, these plans include attendance at a college or university.

Changing Attitudes Toward the Handicapped

Historically, generalized attitudes in our society have impeded the college aspirations and plans of severely disabled individuals. Despite individual differences in the degree of acceptance of handicapped persons, the general climate for disabled persons in our culture is not altogether favorable. [4, 15, 25] Social scientists interested in the welfare of the disabled have been concerned about public attitudes and their modification.

Planned campaigns of community education, the impact of the returning World War II and Korean veterans, and the avoidance of segregation of handicapped persons academically and socially have contributed to an improved public understanding and acceptance of the individual with a serious physical loss. Slowly, at times imperceptibly, increasingly positive community attitudes toward the handicapped are forming. Perceptions of helplessness, avoidance, and rejection are giving way in some cases to constructive acceptance and realistic appreciation of the individual as a totality, not merely as a handicap.

As a result of these changes in attitude, broader opportunities for education and training have been made available to the disabled. One of these opportunities is higher education. If a severely limited student has the intellectual ability and personal qualities which are thought to be related to college success, the community and its professional workers are more likely to consider college attendance for him than they would have been a decade or two ago. As one aspect of our American humanitarian heritage, the growing acceptance of disabled persons as worthy citizens is manifesting itself in a wider belief that they merit college services if otherwise qualified. This belief is apparently being translated into action by educational and rehabilitation officials who are participating in the preparation of disabled youth for college attendance.

Greater Personal Readiness for Admission

More than ever, disabled students are becoming personally ready for college work. Educational and rehabilitation services are being extended with an intensity and comprehensiveness not previously known. In addition, their greater acceptance in the community has encouraged them in their college planning. The community emotional climate for these youth seems to be changing. The process of bringing them out of institutional settings into the local community and their academic and social achievements have made it possible for parents and educators to consider higher education as a possibility for intellectually able youth with severe disabilities [26].

Perhaps the most evident symptom of this change in climate is found in the public high school where the disabled student has ceased to be a curiosity. Many physically handicapped young people now attend the regular high school in the community, participating in extracurricular as well as curricular activities. Teachers and counselors are becoming accustomed to perceiving the handicapped student as a total personality rather than as a handicap somehow attached to a person, with the major emphasis on the handicap. [48] Increasingly, "normal" goals are seen as reasonable for many disabled students. The disabled student who displays superior intellectual ability is likely to be encouraged by his teachers and counselors to consider college attendance.

In part, at least, this acceptance of the handicapped student as possible college "material" is influenced by the changing perception of the role of college education in American life. Enrollments in colleges and universities are rising as increasingly greater proportions of youth enter higher education. Many families consider a college education essential for personal growth, status, and vocational adjustment. This generalized middle-class view of the college as a primary source of development for youth has been • carried over into the area of physical disability. As we have begun to see disabled youth as being fundamentally like nondisabled youth, we have also begun to associate the goals of all youth with them. It has been argued that if college attendance is important for physically "normal" persons, it is equally important for those with physical defects.

Social forces now at work are increasing the present and potential college population in general, and the disabled student population in particular. As the community, the parents, and the students themselves respond to these social influences, it may be expected that the number of handicapped applicants for admission to colleges and universities will continue to increase, perhaps faster than the flow of all other applicants.

PHILOSOPHICAL CONCEPTS RELATING TO THE ADMISSION OF SEVERELY HANDICAPPED STUDENTS

Almost all colleges and universities, at one time or another, have found it necessary to consider applications from severely disabled students. In arriving at both general and individual decisions, many institutions have been influenced by one or more pervading philosophical concepts in our culture—concepts which concern people, their rights and responsibilities in the American culture, and the function of institutions in working with people. Among these concepts are:

1. Any individual who meets college standards of intellectual ability, motivation, and personality adjustment has a right to attend an institution of higher learning. [19]

2. Handicapped students can make contributions to our society that are only partially determined by their physical limitations. In fact, innumerable instances can be cited of outstanding achievements in a large variety of fields by persons with many different handicaps. [14] In the arts, sciences, humanities, and social sciences, contribution after contribution is recorded, often made by persons who had to cope with incredibly difficult physical and personal limitations.

3. In almost all areas of human endeavor today, there is a shortage of skilled professional personnel. Although the shortages in the natural sciences are best known, they are almost equally as critical in other fields. During periods of manpower shortage, America has characteristically turned to special groups for recruits. Along with Negroes and women, the physically handicapped are part of America's underdeveloped personnel resources. This was established during World War II when disabled workers made significant contributions to the defense effort.

In view of the current world economic and political crisis, the United States cannot afford to do without the abilities of all our people. Thus, increasingly, the barriers to college attendance for the intellectually able are being removed. It is hoped in this way not only to express the humanitarian impulses of the nation but to serve the self-interest of our society as well. Using the potentialities of knowledge and skill of physically handicapped youth is one approach which is being suggested to meet the pressing problem of manpower shortages. [28]

4. The college is an institution which should promote individual growth and meet individual needs. The concern for the individual is traditional in higher education in the United States. Since most college curricula provide for individual choices, within limits, counseling is needed to assist the individual to make these choices. Furthermore, the fabric of college life is woven to encourage individual inquiry and thought. More and more we are worried about the plethora of "organization men." Through an individualized approach and an atmosphere of academic freedom for students and teachers, we are attempting to cultivate the unique qualities of each individual.

Many colleges and universities are keyed to an individualized approach. The emphasis, however, has been mainly on intellectual individuality. Yet it is difficult to separate one aspect of individuality from others. A concern for the individual tends to radiate, eventually permeating social, emotional, and physical differences. Many institutions have achieved a degree of consistency. Physical individuality has been perceived by them as just another instance of individuality in general. Once this has been achieved on an ideational level, the next step is usually actual service to physically disabled students.

5. Integration as a value is becoming increasingly evident in education. The earliest education of handicapped children in the United States was highly segregative. During the first half of the nineteenth century, the pattern was set by the establishment of residential schools for deaf and blind children. It was thought that the educational problems of these children were so acute that a full-time controlled setting was necessary. During the last decade of the century, experiments were initiated in day school classes for these children. Gradually, the desirability of having disabled children live with their families was recognized. As the twentieth century dawned, the principle that many severely handicapped children could be educated by the public schools was gaining acceptance. As the mid-century point was reached, an even greater degree of educational and social integration was proposed. It was felt that large numbers of these children could be placed in the regular public school classes in company with nonhandicapped children. The major concession to their educational difference was the possibility that a special itinerant teacher would visit

the class now and then for special work in such areas as communications, special skills, and activities of daily living. [34]

Today, the principle of educational integration for severely disabled children is widely accepted. Any thought that it would be desirable to establish institutions of higher learning for disability groups has been rejected. The consensus is that most disabled students who can meet the academic requirements of college admission should attend the same institutions as their nonhandicapped peers. This is based on a number of reality considerations:

1.   Disabled persons will spend most of their lives in nonsegregated social and occupational situations. Their competence to do so must be heightened by attendance in classes with other students.

2.   It is economically impractical to think of setting up special colleges and universities for disabled students.

3.   With minor modifications, most handicapped students can attend their regular community institutions.

4.   Segregation is a pernicious way of reinforcing and perpetuating exaggerated differences and prejudices.

5.   The academic and social success or failure of a disabled student must lie in the framework of his ability to meet the standards set for other students. A special learning environment would encourage increased dependence on special norms and standards and would enhance the sense of difference between disabled and nondisabled persons in our society.

As the value of integration is acknowledged in racial as well as physical terms, increasing numbers of disabled students are growing up in the company of nondisabled children, being educated with them, and perceiving themselves as capable of attending colleges and universities of their choice, without reference to segregative possibilities. Current emphases on integrated education and rehabilitation stress preparation for living and working in a nonsegregated social environment. One of the aspects of this environment is a nonsegregated college or university.

In summary, the trend in college enrollment of physically limited students is upward. The increase is the result not only of the general increase in college attendance in the population but of special forces within the population of physically handicapped persons. Education and rehabilitation have been liberating forces for this group and have made them increasingly ready for the competition and cooperation demanded in the undergraduate educational institution. The process has also been hastened by changing attitudes within the ranks of handicapped persons as well as among the general public. Disabled persons more often perceive themselves as potential college students and the growing sophistication about physical disability found among educators and the general lay public tends to support and reinforce these feelings. As a result, admissions offices of colleges and universities all over the country may expect an increase in applications from students who are academically prepared for college-level work but who have serious physical handicaps.

A number of philosophical concepts give credence to this movement. As American democracy deepens and spreads, and respect for the individual becomes more widely accepted, these concepts will serve as a continuing stimulus to greater enrollments in colleges and universities of severely physically limited students of good academic ability.

LITERATURE CONCERNING PHYSICALLY HANDICAPPED STUDENTS IN COLLEGES AND UNIVERSITIES

Selected and adequately prepared disabled students have been successful in a wide variety of institutions and curricula in the United States, but most of this evidence lies hidden in the files of institutions, ranging from the smallest to the largest. The students are unheralded and unrecognized. Their exact number cannot even be surmised. The future of their disabilities can only be suggested, yet their numbers run into the thousands. For example, Recording for the Blind (121 East 58th Street, New York 22), a voluntary organization which records textbooks for blind students, numbers some seven hundred college students on its register. Most of these students are absorbed into the ongoing life of the campus, pursuing a course of study without fanfare or special recognition.

The records of state rehabilitation agencies indicate that students with virtually all types of disabilities are attending institutions of higher education. Their success stories become the statistics of state and national agencies. Although relatively little is known of the successes, even less is known of the failures. It is hoped that an extensive survey will be made of this group one day. Current experience seems to indicate that disabled students, as a group, seem to do no worse than other students in their academic achievement.

The literature on the physically handicapped college student can be divided into five major categories: testimonials, philosophical statements, surveys, programs, and follow-up studies. Publications in each of these areas are reviewed below.

Testimonials

These publications consist of informal statements testifying to the advantages to be gained from admitting and serving physically handicapped students to institutions of higher education. Writing from the point of view of the college administrator, Henry [23] reports that the University of Illinois is proud of its pioneer contributions to the education of physically handicapped students. He states that the Illinois experience has led to a better public understanding of the special problems of rehabilitation. Tenny and Stamp [55] report the views of a Wayne State University administrator to the effect that that institution has found it "natural" to make necessary adaptations for the education of capable handicapped students. In the same article, a member of the Wayne teaching staff takes the position that the sincerity, diligence, and achievement of handicapped students amply compensate for the extra attention and time given them. He notes parenthetically that such students require very little extra time.

Strom [53] reports the comments of college administrators about the disabled veterans attending their institutions. Among the points made by these administrators are: (a) Handicapped students have made effective adjustments to their academic programs; (b) the incidence of academic and social difficulties among them is no greater than among other students; and (c) there are no special or unusual problems distinguishing handicapped veterans from nonhandicapped veterans in the college setting.

A final type of testimony comes from disabled persons who have received a college education. For example, Smithdas [52], a deaf-blind person, describes his undergraduate and graduate experiences in two New York City institutions. Baer [3] reports on the special problems of a student in a wheel chair attending college. Many of these experiences are discussed in biographies and autobiographies of disabled individuals. As a group, they tend to give testimony to the ability of severely disabled individuals to profit from college attendance.

Philosophical Statements

Various writers on the education and rehabilitation of physically disabled persons have examined the college experience from a philosophical point of view. For example, both Weir [61] and Fleischer [19] see real possibilities for severely disabled persons in college programs. However, both stress the need for adequate selection, guidance, and preparation.

Surveys

The survey method has been widely used, both with institutions and individuals, to ascertain the status and problems of physically handicapped students in American colleges and universities. In 1944, Gitnick [23] conducted one of the early surveys of this type. On the basis of questionnaire responses from 320 colleges and universities, she found that only two institutions (both of them military schools) definitely did not accept physically handicapped students. However, many of the respondents refused to accept students with certain types of disabilities. In many instances, the responses were ambiguous, reflecting the lack of a firm policy about the admission of disabled students. Among the institutions surveyed, only 5 per cent had adequate elevator service; 2 to 3 per cent had ramps; 14 per cent had hand rails in their buildings; and less than 2 per cent provided campus parking facilities for disabled students. Gitnick found that the responding colleges and universities reviewed the applications of disabled students more carefully than other applications. She reports that 44 per cent of the institutions had no records of the number of physically handicapped students in attendance. Gitnick concludes that most of the colleges and universities included in the study were not equipped to serve severely disabled students.

Zundell [68], in a survey conducted in 1952, reports on the policies and practices of 119 colleges and universities responding to her questionnaire. Although eight years had elapsed since Gitnick's study, the findings presented by Zundell closely approximate those reported in the earlier paper. Zundell found that very few colleges had the physical facilities which would have made attendance possible by severely disabled students. Two-thirds of the colleges in this sample had buildings without ramps or elevators. Although only a small minority of the respondents excluded physically disabled students altogether, many lacked a definite policy. Even among the institutions accepting disabled students, Zundell found that the arrangements made for them were informal and almost makeshift. Few of the institutions made any effort to accommodate severely handicapped students. Zundell agrees with Gitnick's earlier conclusion that facilities in many of these institutions would have to be improved if physically disabled students were to attend.

In 1957, Condon [8] reported the results of a questionnaire survey based on responses from 181 colleges. Thirty-one of these respondents indicated that they maintained an organized service program for physically handicapped students. Another 105 respondents reported that, although they maintained no special organized program, they did offer some services to this group. Forty-five colleges offered neither special programs nor special services. Those serving disabled students reported that they identified such students through information received from "feeding" high schools and from physical examinations given incoming freshmen. After gaining admission, disabled students were not required to meet any special standards or stipulations. Most of the colleges admitted such students only after consultation within the institution with representatives of the college medical office, the registrar's office, and the office of the dean of students.

In the same study, Condon found that only one out of four institutions surveyed had physical facilities which favored the admission of students on crutches and in wheel chairs. The respondent colleges reported a number of adjustments which facilitated attendance by severely disabled students. Among these were special elevator passes, early class dismissal to avoid "rush" periods, special examination procedures, and permission to use some special devices such as recording machines and braille slates in the classrooms. With the exception of cerebral palsied students, most severely disabled individuals were encouraged to participate in the regular extracurricular programs of the responding institutions. Condon concludes that, with the assistance of agencies for the handicapped, most colleges could develop effective programs for serving this group. She sees value in these students attending the same institutions as other students and points up the benefits to be gained by providing them with specialized counseling services. She feels that such counseling should encourage student independence, insofar as possible.

The foregoing surveys were attempts to study handicapped college students on a broad base, examining the procedures used in many institutions for handling a variety of disabilities. Other surveys have been devoted to the attainment of more limited goals. Strom [53] studied the experiences of 453 colleges and universities serving physically handicapped veterans of World War II. He found that the institutions tended to have favorable attitudes toward these students. The most common forms of special assistance provided were transportation facilities (special parking privileges, elevators, and ramps), housing arrangements (special dormitory facilities and preference in referral to private boardinghouses near campus), classroom adjustments (special scheduling of classes, waiving of some prerequisites, substitutions of equivalent courses, and use of special equipment in the classroom), and student personnel and counseling programs. In the same study, Strom interviewed 391 disabled veterans studying on 39 colleges campuses. He concludes that most disabled veteran college students adapted to the college environment and that, with the exception of a small minority, these students were having academic, financial, and personal problems not dissimilar from those of other students. He found that they asked for and needed relatively few special services.

Abraham [1] received questionnaire responses from 90 colleges and universities concerning procedures used with epileptic students. Nine per cent of these institutions generally accepted epileptics; 46 per cent accepted them conditionally; 2 per cent admitted them reluctantly; 34 per cent had no regulations for this group; and 9 per cent failed to respond. Two-thirds of the responding institutions believe that the possibility of seizures should limit the student's educational program—14 per cent seriously, 18 per cent moderately, and 35 per cent slightly. Abraham concludes that some colleges and universities do not provide equal educational opportunities for epileptics. He suggests that both faculties and student bodies could benefit from programs designed to educate them about epilepsy.

Condon [9] studied the attitudes of New York State colleges and universities toward blind students. She found that 24 of her 98 responding institutions were currently enrolling 54 blind students. All 24 institutions offered reader services to blind students. Sixteen cooperated with outside agencies to provide tape recordings of textbooks; 10 made typewriters available; 19 made provision for examinations to be given by readers; 6 provided reading cubicles; and 3 maintained soundproof reading rooms. In all 24 institutions, blind students attended the regular classes and were expected to measure up to the standards maintained for all students.

Schweikert [51] conducted a study of college and university practices relating to students in wheel chairs. He found that 427 wheel-chair students were in attendance at 76 colleges. One hundred and thirty-four colleges were analyzed relative to the adequacy of their facilities for wheel-chair students. Only 13 were found to offer little or no difficulty to such students insofar as physical facilities were concerned. Thirty-eight were limited to some degree and 79 were inadequate. Schweikert found that a number of institutions were deeply interested in eliminating as many barriers as possible. A trend toward considering the needs of disabled students was noted in the planning of new college buildings.

It should be noted that the earlier surveys suggest the existence of more stringent limitations on physically handicapped college students than do the later ones. The trend seems to be toward more liberal admission policies and broader service programs.

Programs

Program descriptions in the literature may be divided into two major types: those reporting actual programs in action and those suggesting desirable programs recommended for adoption by one or more institutions. Several publications report on the first type. The special program for physically disabled students at the University of Illinois has been described in news items appearing in such journals as *Rehabilitation Literature* [27], *Sigma Signs* [14], and the *Crippled Child* [62]. In 1959, *Sigma Signs* reported that 128 disabled students were associated with the University of Illinois Student Rehabilitation Center, a facility offering therapy and counseling services. This Center functions as a coordinating body, assisting the University to understand and provide for its severely handicapped enrollees. Among its achievements have been the provision of ramps, making all University buildings accessible to handicapped students, the addition of two buses with hydraulic equipment which make hourly trips around the campus to transport severely disabled students, and the scheduling of physical therapy classes, replacing standard physical education classes for selected disabled students.

Fife [18] describes the program at Southern Illinois University. In 1960, this program served 63 severely disabled individuals, including 11 blind students, 8 deaf students, and 32 students who were in wheel chairs or had severe mobility limitations. Among the services offered to these students are changes in classroom assignments if necessary, reading rooms for blind students, modified dormitory rooms with wider doors suitable for students in wheel chairs, modified sidewalk routes, and breaks in the curbing. A special orientation to the campus is given to blind students. Some disabled students are permitted to use their own cars on campus and are provided with special parking permits. The University has established a clinical center where students receive physical therapy, counseling and psychotherapy, hearing diagnosis, and speech correction. Special competitive sports activities are conducted for disabled students. Under certain circumstances, very severely disabled students are allowed to have an attendant while studying at the University.

Kottke [35], after offering evidence of the importance of a college education to disabled students, cites cases illustrating some of the experience gained at the University of Minnesota. Kottke's special emphasis is on the role of the college physician in a program for handicapped students. Heldberg and Aaronson [32] report on a counseling program for disabled veterans at the same Institution. Through the University of Minnesota Bureau of Veterans Affairs, college counselors cooperated with the Veterans Administration to provide essential services to disabled students, including admissions counseling, testing and advisement, supervision of training, and termination of the college experience. Although the program described was limited to veterans, the authors suggest that a similar program would be suitable for disabled non-veterans. They feel that the success of the program was due, in part, to a centralization of responsibility and to a sensitivity to the campus problems of disabled students.

Condon [11] describes the development of the Health Guidance Board at the College of the City of New York. This Board serves as a coordinating body for services to physically handicapped students, assisting them with problems of admissions, registration, and class attendance. Among the specific problems for which help is given are special conditions for taking examinations, obtaining readers and tutors, and participation in extracurricular activities. A feature of this program is the close working relationship developed with community agencies.

Two highly specialized programs are discussed by Gamble [20] and Harrison and Cantoni [30]. Gamble describes the unique teaching-by-telephone program offered at Boston University, a program designed to serve students who are so disabled that physical attendance at college is impossible. In a similar vein, Harrison and Cantoni report the use of correspondence study by severely disabled persons. Most of their experience has been with tuberculosis patients in sanitariums. Under these circumstances, correspondence study has been a useful rehabilitation tool.

The second series of program papers suggest recommended techniques and provisions for disabled college students. Condon and Lerner [12] describe the college counselor serving the handicapped as a rehabilitation worker. The authors discuss the rehabilitation implications of counselor functions in admissions, faculty contacts, student counseling, and cooperation with community agencies. Hardee [29] also stresses the cooperative relationship between the college counselor and the community rehabilitation agency. She suggests that rehabilitation agency personnel should become more familiar with the college environment and should develop better communication with college counselors.

McGill and Frisch [39] discuss the problems of preparing blind students for college attendance, describing a program conducted at the Chicago Lighthouse. Prospective blind college students spent two weeks during the summer in a preparatory program that stressed study habits, personal social development, and improved understanding of college procedures. Finally, Stuart [54] reports on the development of an objective rating scale useful in evaluating readiness for college attendance. This approach requires an analysis of the demands of various college courses and buildings and an evaluation of student capacities. The process is related to that developed for use in the selective placement of physically disabled workers. Stuart indicates that the success of similar procedures in placement suggest that they will be useful in the college setting as well.

Follow-up Studies

Colleges and universities are often interested in ascertaining the post-college experience of all their graduates. However, several specialized studies have been published reporting the degree of success achieved by physically handicapped alumni. Condon [10] followed 159 individuals who had been enrolled in the College of the City of New York and had received special services for the physically handicapped. Condon found that her respondents were employed in a wide variety of jobs. With the exception of the cerebral palsied subgroup, they were earning salaries comparable to those earned by nondisabled persons employed in similar jobs. Condon concludes that, if given the requisite educational opportunities, the physically handicapped college-trained person can compete successfully in the occupational world.

Mase and Williams [38] conducted a follow-up study of 243 severely handicapped college graduates in an effort to assess the college experience of this group. When comparisons were made with nonhandicapped college graduates, the authors found that there were no differences between the two groups in occupational success and emotional adjustment.

Lerner and Martin [36] present follow-up data on 59 disabled graduates and students of Hunter College, New York. Forty-eight of these disabled subjects were rated as academically successful. It was found that only 5 per cent of the handicapped students enrolled at Hunter College were dropped for poor scholarship. As a matter of fact, Lerner notes that the prospects for graduation of her sample were greater than for entering freshmen as a group. Lerner concludes that, if given suitable and adequate college services, severely handicapped students can achieve satisfactorily in college and employment.

This summary of the literature suggests that some colleges and universities have compiled an extensive body of experience in serving physically disabled students. In almost all cases, the reports of this experience are favorable. Evidently many institutions have admitted disabled students with gratifying results. While the reports and studies reviewed lack precision and proper controls, the trend of the data is sufficiently consistent to suggest that the conclusions reached have some degree of validity. One of the major needs in this area is for more adequate surveys and control studies of disabled college students. As increasing numbers of disabled students enter the colleges and universities, and as additional research funds become available for studies of this type, further data should be forthcoming.

The available evidence indicates that colleges and universities will be asked to serve growing numbers of severely disabled students in the next decade. In the absence of a definitive literature, these institutions may suffer from a lack of guidance in managing the problems of such students. As a result, the author will attempt in the succeeding chapters to draw on his observations and experience to delineate some of the problems and to highlight some of the issues in this field. The opinions expressed should be accepted as personal, to be tested by later experimentation. At this time, they constitute a working guide, subject to possible change as the data are accumulated and insights develop.

2

Facilities for the Physically Handicapped College Student

IN EDUCATION for the severely disabled student, the college administrator and the student have a common problem. Both wonder if the college campus will have the physical facilities necessary to meet the needs of a person with a particular limitation. Often the question is raised, "Can this college accommodate a totally blind student?" This question is repeated many times, substituting deafness, orthopedic handicap, epilepsy, or almost any other disease entity for blindness. Although it is impossible to provide definitive answers that cover all campuses and all students, a few principles emerge.

Disabled students are individual. Merely classifying a student as visually or aurally handicapped, post-polio or cerebral palsied, diabetic or tubercular, provides little descriptive data about him. Individuality of adaptation and response to disability is the general rule to such a degree that persons having the same objective degree of limitation from the same cause may function quite differently from each other. Not all above-the-knee amputees with peripheral vascular disease adjust similarly to a leg prosthesis. Some are quite adequate on their artificial limbs and require minimal special services on a college campus. Others find it impossible to use the limb at all or only with great difficulty. Consequently, in discussing the physical facilities required for *a* disabled student, generalizations can be used only as guidelines. The college has a responsibility to avoid stereotyping the individual. Through techniques described in the next chapter, it must analyze the individual's capacities and measure them against the physical demands of its academic and campus life.

24

Most college campuses have within them the physical resources to meet the needs of most disabled students. In the last century, it was fashionable to think of the problems of disabled persons in terms of custom-made environments. Thus, in educating physically handicapped children, the residential school and its made-to-order facilities were regarded with considerable favor. It was believed that the needs of blind, deaf, and orthopedically handicapped children were so unique that special engineering was needed to construct facilities for them. Some of this thinking still prevails. Looking about their campuses, administrators and faculty members may see innumerable barriers to the attendance of severely disabled sudents. In considering the possible acceptance of such young people into the institution, they may be appalled at the possible sources of safety hazard, the barriers to free and easy mobility, and the physical inadequacies of their own plants.

One institution hesitated to admit deaf students because traffic conditions on the campus constituted unusual safety hazards even for normally hearing students. It was thought that the inability to hear automobile horns and other sounds would accentuate this hazard to such a degree that it was unwise to accept most deaf applicants for admission. In another case, a college was unusually cautious in accepting blind students because it was believed that its hilly campus could not be safely traversed by a blind person walking without aid. There is no doubt that there are reality factors on most campuses which make their use by physically disabled students questionable. However, these physical features should be examined scientifically to determine if they really constitute an undesirable environment for the severely handicapped student or if they are, to some degree, a focus of unrealistic attitudes toward such students.

Let us examine the two instances in the last paragraph. Deaf persons throughout the world are functioning in communities which use sound symbols extensively. Failure to hear these stimuli does, in some instances, create life-adjustment problems for the deaf individual. Yet these problems can be magnified and distorted. Most hearing individuals are, themselves, from time to time temporarily deaf to such stimuli as they walk the streets, unaware of much of the physical environment, lost in their thoughts. One can only wonder if the accident rate would materially rise if all automobile horns were silenced. As part of its anti-noise campaign, New York City has made the sounding of automobile horns illegal except in emergencies. Yet street accidents are no more numerous than they were when New Yorkers were sounding their horns at each other at the least provocation. Actually, as part of their education and rehabilitation, deaf persons are trained to rely more heavily on visual stimuli. There is no evidence to suggest that deaf persons suffer a higher incidence of street accidents than other groups in the community.

The evidence bearing on the blind student and the hilly campus is equally worth attention. Given proper training in orientation and mobility, most blind students would have minor difficulties, if any, on a campus used by seeing persons, however hilly. It is true that some special attention would have to be given to this student initially. A representative of the staff or the student body would have to assist him during the first few days on campus in becoming oriented to the physical plant. Once this was accomplished, the blind student should be able to function quite adequately in most campus situations. With such assistance, blind students are safely navigating such diverse environments as the traffic maze of lower Manhattan, the hills of San Francisco, and the traffic conditions of Mexico City. There is sometimes a tendency for the nondisabled person to identify with the situation of the handicapped person and to visualize his own inadequacy in a like situation.

Disabled students often have great capacity for adaptation. Almost any campus could be redesigned to make it more comfortable for disabled young people. The salient fact, however, is that these young people will be required to spend their lives in physical environments which were built on the premise of normal physical capacity. There is little likelihood that communities will undertake major changes to make their resources more accessible to the physically handicapped. It would be unrealistic to expect Braille signs in our cities to guide blind persons, or the use of printed titles on sound motion pictures to help deaf persons with lip-reading problems. It would be equally unrealistic to believe that college campuses will make substantial modifications.

It is an interesting fact that many disabled persons would not want these changes made. They have been prepared to live under conditions which may not favor them but which are the normal ones in our society. In most cases, they expect to make necessary adaptations, the extent and range of which sometimes startle the lay person. One wonders how a blind person can learn so much in a classroom when the visual stimuli of the blackboard, the illustrations, and the facial expression of the lecturer are inaccessible to him. Yet, for many years, radio drama and lectures were appreciated by most Americans. To all intents and purposes, the listener to radio, tape recordings, and phonograph records is blind.

Most of us use our faculties to a degree less than their potentialities would suggest. The disabled student, having lost some of his physical capacities, still retains vast resources which can be used to offset some of the losses. Workers in the fields of special education and rehabilitation specialize in helping disabled persons to develop their residual strengths and abilities, thus lessening the effects of the particular physical loss.

Even if a college campus does present substantial problems to a disabled student, he may, with proper assistance, find ways to handle them successfully. In some cases, the problems are so serious and uncompromising that little can be done to help him, but these constitute a small minority. In most instances, given an opportunity to try himself out in the situation, and professional assistance in learning to live within the limitations of the environment, the disabled student will find ways of overcoming at least a part of the difficulty confronting him. In essence, this constitutes a caution for college administrators and faculties. Even if a student initially gives evidence of lacking the capacity to fit into the physical requirements of the campus, it is often helpful to consult with rehabilitation specialists to determine if the perceived limitation is inflexible. Oftentimes, professional rehabilitation counselors suggest special types of training or minor changes in the environment which make it possible for a student to meet the physical demands of the campus.

Some of the special needs of persons with certain types of disabilities will be identified in the sections that follow. However, this discussion should not be interpreted as indicating that the lack of these facilities necessarily means that such students should be excluded from a campus. Acceptance or exclusion should be based on a careful study of each disabled applicant. There is no formula that can be used in assessing an individual. All that can be offered are *desirable* conditions for each group. Desirability should not be equated with essentiality. Many handicapped students in a particular disability category function successfully despite the absence of one or more of the favorable conditions discussed in the pages that follow. In any case, the significant variable is the total individual, not the name of his disability. With this thought firmly in mind, some of the conditions which may be helpful to persons with particular disabilities can be discussed. In fact, it should be noted that the conditions listed are favorable to all students. Good lighting in a college not only assists the partially seeing person, but contributes to his fully sighted colleague as well.

THE BLIND STUDENT

No adjustments in the physical features of the campus will be required by the properly trained blind student.

The blind student will be helped if recordings of some of his textbooks are made available to him. However, this is arranged by the student himself. The organization most frequently used for this purpose is Recording for the Blind, but there are other similar service groups. Ordinarily, as early as possible the student ascertains the names of his texts for the coming semester and purchases or borrows the books and mails them to the office of the recording service. Under favorable circumstances, he will have part or all of his materials transcribed on records by the time the new semester begins. This service is provided without fee. The finished records may be played on a Talking Book Machine or a similar phonograph which accommodates discs to be played at 16 2/3 revolutions per minute. Many blind students already own such machines or have received them from the United States Library of Congress, without cost.

Supplementary reading and library research present a more difficult problem. A number of states grant stipends to blind students so that they may employ seeing readers, usually other college students who are taking the same courses or are advanced students in the same area of study. The blind student may need some assistance in locating such readers on the campus, but there are many seeing students who regard this as a satisfactory way of earning additional income and are eager for assignments. The college can be of help by merely listing the job opening in its placement bureau and referring candidates to the blind student for interview. Another area of college responsibility is locating and assigning space in the library where the student and his reader may work with a minimum of interruption. Often, any quiet room will do. If this can be arranged, the whole range of college library materials will be at the disposal of the blind student.

Braille is less often used for reading by college students than once was the case. There is an increasingly heavy reliance on recorded books. However, Braille remains an essential tool for the blind student. Some attempts have been made to use tape recorders for note-taking, but this technique is still in the experimental stage. Most blind students will have to rely on Braille for their notes. Braille writing is performed on a metal slate. Using a Braille stylus, the blind student taps out the Braille characters which serve as his notes. Actually, there is only one minor difference between note-taking activities of blind and seeing students. The former, in their use of Braille, are likely to produce audible sounds as they record their notes. The sound of the stylus embossing the Braille dots into the relatively thick paper creates a characteristic tapping sound. A few instructors continue to be disturbed by the sound, even after the student has been in class for some time, but usually they soon become accustomed to it without special effort. If Braille note-taking causes tension in the teacher, it may be well to assign the student to another instructor or to arrange for him to take his notes through another medium. Although the latter is less feasible, some alternatives are possible.

A seeing student may make a carbon copy of his notes. This method is less desirable since it increases the blind student's dependence on others, makes him rely on another person's selective note-taking which may or may not focus on the same concepts and information as he himself would record, and such notes are accessible to him only through having someone else read them to him. On the other hand, Braille is the direct product of his own learning activity, accessible to him whenever he wishes.

Some blind students take no written notes at all. Through making more efficient use of memory, they may actually recall a good deal of the material. However, reliance on memory is less satisfactory than active note-taking. It makes the listening learner more passive, giving him fewer opportunities to relate himself dynamically to the class materials. A blind student's decision to refrain from note-taking should be a last resort. It should never be because the student lacks the techniques for doing so. It is justified only as an emergency measure.

The mobility techniques used by well-prepared blind students generally do not demand adjustments in the college environment. Most students use canes, if they lack sufficient residual vision to travel without aid. In some instances, a guide dog may be used. If the dog has been provided by an established guide dog organization, it may be assumed that both the dog and the master have been trained to function together in ways which will cause no disruption on the campus. The guide dog usually attends classes with his master and will probably lie next to him, requiring virtually no attention. Initially, the blind student may need assistance in setting up a routine for walking his dog in places approved by the institution. In no other way should the dog create special hazards or sanitary problems for the college. Occasionally, the dog's illness or a disturbance in the student-dog relationship may create a temporary problem. The student is trained to recognize such a problem and to seek professional help, when indicated.

Most legally blind students cannot see well enough to benefit from extensive blackboard work. If such work is in the context of a typical lecture-recitation course, the blind student can usually follow the accompanying explanation. He is often helped by a deliberate attempt on the instructor's part to make his verbal explanation of the blackboard or other visual materials more detailed and descriptive. Many instructors respond to this need positively. In doing so, they sometimes find that the technique is also helpful to other students. In some courses, such as mathematics, blackboard work is critical, and the student may need tutorial assistance before and after class to properly grasp the subject matter presented on the board. This help may be given by mathematics majors serving as volunteers or as paid readers for the blind student. In any event, it should be noted that many blind students function successfully in college mathematics; some have even majored in mathematics. At least one instance has been recorded of a totally blind person having become a mathematics professor at a leading university.

Some colleges and universities have established language laboratories in which tapes and other recording materials are widely used. Taped work is also used experimentally in a number of other courses. Obviously, the blind student is at no disadvantage in this instance. In the use of television, however, when the teaching materials are significantly visual in character, the problem may be more complex. The blind student may grasp the necessary understanding just from the verbal portion of the telecast, or he may need a running description from a seeing student or from the instructor. If this is done quietly it should cause only a minimum disturbance to other students. If it does annoy others, arrangements should be made for the blind student and a colleague to see the telecast in another room.

Typewriters are basic tools for blind students, and most of them own their own machines and are trained touch typists. The only problem which arises in their use is at examination or quiz time. Many blind students prefer to take essay tests on the typewriter but the noise of the machine may distract other students. It may be necessary to secure a private working space for the blind student in which he can type without disturbing others. All that is needed is for a seeing person to read the questions to the student who will probably take Braille notes as the questions are read so that he can refer to them later. Once this is done, the blind student is usually independent.

Objective test questions are handled quite easily. At the time that the examination is given to the rest of the class the blind student receives a copy of the examination paper and then retires with his reader to a space assigned to them. The reader reads the questions and records the blind student's responses. It is possible that the blind student will need a time extension since this method of taking a test is relatively time-consuming.

This amount of space has been devoted to the adjustments required by blind students because they are often thought to be very seriously disabled in relation to college work. Yet most colleges and universities have enrolled some blind students and have found that, as a group, they tend to achieve as well as other students. Even though some modifications in study techniques are necessary, performance standards can be retained intact.

THE PARTIALLY SEEING STUDENT

Partially seeing students have visual impairments which are much less serious than blindness. They retain enough useful vision so that sight can be used to a great degree in the educational process. In fact, many of them are fully capable of reading for varying periods of time. However, the nature of the eye condition and the possibility of further impairment of vision may make them less able than other students to perform close work for the periods of time required by the usual college curriculum. Some of the adjustments they need are applicable to only a small proportion of the group. The partially seeing include a wide variety of visual acuities, limitations, and diagnoses. The aids indicated below may help some members of the group but serve as a deterrent to others. For example, many partially seeing students are helped by brighter than ordinary classroom lighting of a desired type; others who have retinitis pigmentosa or albinism may actually feel more comfortable with less light. Thus, among the partially seeing, as with all groups discussed in this chapter, adjustments must be individual. The applicability of each of the factors described below can be determined only through consultation with an eye specialist.

Some partially seeing students are overwhelmed by the reading requirements of a college curriculum, and performing these assignments may actually be deleterious to their remaining vision. In other cases, even though such a danger does not exist, extended periods of reading cause headaches, blurring of vision, dizziness, and other discomfort. In these cases, the student will have to rely on a seeing reader or electronic recordings, or he may have to reduce his program. If special reading aids are indicated, this will be a matter between the student and his family and/or rehabilitation counselor. The college usually does not enter into such arrangements. If a reduced program is suggested, the institution may decide the limits to be set on such a program. Many institutions will permit these students to take ten or twelve credits per semester. A few will agree to more radically reduced loads. If the minimum academic load permitted by the college is still too demanding upon the student visually, he may have to withdraw from the institution or obtain rehabilitation services which may better prepare him to meet the physical demands of college study.

Classroom lighting can be highly important to a partially seeing student. The regular classroom may have too much light or glare for a student in this group, or the lighting may be too dim for him. Some institutions attempt to schedule the classes in which a partially seeing student is enrolled in classrooms which best meet his needs. But this often constitutes a complex administrative problem requiring a level of individual attention which exceeds what the college is ready to provide.

Almost invariably, the partially seeing student will have to adjust to the lighting conditions that exist in his classrooms. However, a few simple adaptations may be helpful. If classroom lighting is too bright, the student may wear medically approved tinted lenses. If the light is too dim, the instructor may seat the student in the best lighted section of the room, and as close to the blackboard as possible. Sometimes, a student will be permitted to bring certain aids to class. These may include small lamps, magnifiers, and special optical aids such as microscopic lenses.

Large-type materials are widely used for partially seeing students in elementary schools. In the lower grades, books printed in larger than ordinary type sizes and in highly readable type faces on nonglare paper perform a valuable service in the special education of partially seeing students. In secondary schools, fewer of these materials are available. Often, they must be prepared through individual means, by use of typewriters with large clear type faces. While the partially seeing child is in school, his teachers, parents, or others may prepare materials for him in this way. At the college level, this approach is less feasible. The mass of material is so voluminous that even extensive efforts in this direction will make only a small dent in the mass of reading that has to be done. A more realistic substitute is the use of electronic recordings. With the assistance of rehabilitation workers, partially seeing students may arrange to have a large part of their reading assignments placed on tapes or discs.

In most respects, the partially seeing student creates few special problems on the college campus. He may be exposed to a certain degree of social tension, having more than his share of mistaken identities, misinterpretation of visual cues, and difficulties in functioning in certain sports. These are not crucial in most cases. However, special educators and rehabilitation counselors have probably worked on some of these problems with him. They may appear to be a more serious problem to the casual observer than to the student himself.

THE DEAF STUDENT

Deaf students are those who do not use hearing in the learning process. The physical loss in this group occurred prior to the acquisition of language. As a result, both speech and language were learned through special instruction in childhood and adolescence. Their speech, although often readily understood, has a characteristic quality to it. In some cases, the language handicap persists throughout life. In college, they may function through spoken communication and lip reading supplemented by the writing of messages, when necessary. The following facilities may be helpful to many deaf students.

Language assessment at the time of admission is highly desirable. Through the use of reading and other language tests, every effort should be made to ascertain the current language development of the deaf student. In view of the fact that much college-level learning takes place through the medium of words, serious language deficiencies can constitute major handicaps in the college curriculum. Some deaf persons achieve word fluency of a high order. Others do not. The latter group may need remedial work prior to entrance into college or assistance in developing other educational and vocational plans. For some deaf students, the language handicap can be more restricting at the higher educational levels than the absence of hearing, per se.

A good deal of college learning takes place on an abstract level. Much of it is in the realm of ideation and concept formation. As a group, deaf students tend to function best in concrete situations in which direct experience is possible. Numerous deaf young people are able to surmount this problem and function quite successfully in the areas of abstraction required in college work. Others, however, may have profound difficulties in this area. As a result, in working with deaf students, the testing services of a college or university can be helpful in assessing the student's ability to work in the realm of abstraction. In cases in which evaluation results are doubtful or negative, it would be wise for college personnel to consult psychologists who specialize in working with deaf individuals. In this way, the approximate capacities and limitations may be better understood and may serve more effectively as a basis for institutional planning for the student.

Some deaf students are skillful lip readers. Even at best, however, lip reading is an imperfect tool. Only a proportion of the necessary cues can be quickly and accurately identified. In many instances, the deaf student has to fill in numerous gaps through his familiarity with the context of the conversation. On occasion, he fails to interpret adequately, committing educational and social errors. The likelihood of such misinterpretations is enhanced by technical subject matter, unfamiliar subject areas, and courses in foreign languages in which a totally new language context has to be learned. Obviously, lip reading does not fully compensate for the loss of hearing. Yet, despite the fact that a number of deaf students find it most expedient to enroll in Gallaudet College in Washington, D.C., an institution of higher education for deaf students, some do enroll in regular colleges and universities. In fact, there are recorded instances of individuals successfully managing college-level work despite deafness and blindness. Helen Keller is an example of such an individual.

The college can assist the deaf student in his lip-reading problems to some degree. Good lighting makes lip reading easier. Whenever possible, the deaf student should be assigned to classrooms where brighter lighting has been installed. He will function best if seated where he can see the lips of the instructor. Teachers who move about the room frequently and turn their backs to sections of the class group present greater difficulty to the deaf student. The instructor whose lips can be readily seen and perceived simplifies the task of the deaf student. Classes which involve a rapid give and take of discussion constitute areas of difficulty. Lip reading, at best, is a difficult process. The deaf student soon learns to identify the individuals on the faculty whom he can read best. Assignment to those individuals, whenever possible, can contribute to the ultimate academic success of a deaf student.

Speech is often a lifelong problem for the deaf student. Never having heard sound, speech is for him a painfully learned skill that is subject to alteration and deterioration unless constantly checked and practiced. Even the imperfect speech of many deaf persons represents a great learning achievement. Throughout the school years, speech instruction has aimed not only at teaching him an acceptable level of speech, but also at maintaining current levels of verbal communication. The deaf student at college must rely heavily on his speech. Yet he lacks the hearing which serves as a constant corrective for human speech. Without special facilities, his speech becomes less useful to him. A speech center or a similar facility can help the deaf student preserve and improve his speech. In the absence of a college-sponsored facility, a community speech center or a private speech therapist may be helpful. If none of these facilities is available, the deaf student will run some risk of speech deterioration.

Owing to language and lip-reading problems, deaf students sometimes miss essential concepts presented in the classroom. They often need tutoring assistance to forestall the permanent effect of such learning gaps. Many courses are cumulative. Today's work may rest on the foundations laid yesterday. Inability to grasp fully the ideas of one session may mean inability to grasp the concepts of the next, and so a vicious cycle is set in motion. Working daily with advanced students in certain areas of the curriculum enables many deaf students to keep up to date in their work. Although the use of tutors in this way must be financed by other educational and rehabilitation agencies, the college can help the student locate effective tutoring help and should orient the faculty to this special problem.

The deaf student falls into the category of those with nonvisible disabilities. Casual observers on the campus may not perceive the student as handicapped. His lack of response to sound stimuli may be variously misinterpreted as preoccupation with other matters, lack of awareness, or disinclination to respond. In an official sense, college admissions officers, medical staff, and student personnel workers are responsible for notifying the faculty and administrative officers of the student's situation. The student and his counselor will work out ways to handle the disability in social and academic situations which require interpretation by the student himself.

There are enough instances of deaf students succeeding in college to warrant optimism. Often the key to the situation is careful selection of the deaf student, providing conditions which will maximize his lip-reading abilities, and assisting the faculty to understand his learning problems.

THE HARD-OF-HEARING STUDENT

The hard-of-hearing student uses his aural sense for learning. However, his hearing acuity, even with the correction of a hearing aid, is sufficiently impaired to constitute a learning barrier. These students have learned language at least partially through hearing so that it is less of a problem for them than for deaf students. Some of them depend on lip reading as an aid in understanding speech. Lip reading is thus important for communication, even when used without training or conscious effort. Under proper conditions, some hard-of-hearing students can function in a hearing environment fairly well. Others have constant difficulty. In either event, certain adjustments in the college environment can be exceedingly helpful.

For hard-of-hearing students who are assisted by lip reading, the adjustments noted in the section on deaf students are equally applicable. If a counselor or a faculty member finds that such a student is using lip reading with only modest success, it may be advisable to refer him for an evaluation by a hearing rehabilitation specialist. Often, these students can benefit from professional speech and hearing therapy. Increased lip-reading facility may make a material change in academic achievement and social success.

Hard-of-hearing students who rely on hearing aids may find that certain types of acoustic environments are more favorable than others. For example, a profusion of external noises—traffic, other students conversing in the halls, noisy air conditioners, and the like—may reduce hearing efficiency. As a result, it is important to ascertain from the hard-of-hearing student the conditions which favor maximum hearing effectiveness. Wherever possible, he should be helped by being placed in an environment which approximates these favorable conditions.

A student with a hearing loss in the high frequencies may discover that he hears certain voices better than others. Perhaps a deep male voice is more easily perceived than a fragile high-pitched female voice. If this is the case, some consideration should be given to the selection of instructors. Naturally, this type of scheduling is possible only when there are multiple sections of a course, taught by different instructors.

In teaching and counseling, it is essential for college personnel to be reasonably sure that the student has heard them. At times, it may seem superficially that this has been the case. Subsequently, however, it may appear that this was not so. As a result, staff members working with severely limited hard-of-hearing students need to do more than make a conscious effort to be clear in their speech. They also should ascertain through pointed questions if the student has grasped the materials. If necessary, they should repeat their statements, perhaps in different ways, until it seems likely that communication has been established.

THE STUDENT IN A WHEEL CHAIR

Students with exceedingly limiting orthopedic and neurological disabilities may depend on the wheel chair as the major aid to mobility. Among disease entities which result in such dependence are poliomyelitis, paraplegia, cerebral palsy, diseases of the nervous system, strokes, and amputations. Living in a wheel chair presents numerous difficult problems. Among them are the mechanics of daily living, inability to enter some buildings because of steps, inaccessibility of many means of public transportation, and inability to participate in such activities as walking, dancing, and sports. Sometimes the illness which has necessitated the use of the wheel chair may have impaired arms, shoulders, and/or hands, resulting in partial or very limited ability to handle one's own wheel chair. In such cases, dependence on others is even greater.

A few institutions have attracted large numbers of wheel-chair cases as a result of making changes in their environments. For most institutions, the problem is one of admitting and serving a very small group of wheel-chair students. A number of these institutions have found that the problems were less imposing than had been anticipated. Capitalizing on features in their plant which had previously been little noticed, they were able to accommodate some of these students. For example, one institution had believed that all its entrances required the mounting of steps. Subsequently it was discovered that almost every building had a delivery entrance which was flush with the ground. Another institution rejected students in wheel chairs because some of the classes were held on the second floors of its buildings. There were no elevators in these structures. Later, it was discovered that more than 85 per cent of the classes were held in first-floor classrooms and that it was possible to plan an academic program for a student in a wheel chair without making major alterations in plant or academic structure. Discussed below are a few features in a college plant which will be helpful to students in wheel chairs. There are instances on record where institutions lacked one or more of these and yet succeeded in providing a good educational program for a chair-bound student.

To benefit from the college program, wheel-chair students must have access to the buildings in which essential college activities are housed. Thus, a student's inability to enter the gymnasium or the observatory may be relatively less significant than a similar incapacity in relation to classrooms, offices, and certain science laboratories. It is essential that wheel-chair students be able to enter and leave such buildings with a minimum of assistance. Naturally, an entrance level with the ground is highly desirable but somewhat rare. Usually one or more steps lead to the entrances of most older college buildings. If delivery entrances cannot be used, and if the flights of steps are fairly low, ramps are often successful in meeting the problem. The college maintenance staff can construct these out of odd pieces of lumber with a minimum investment of time. If possible, a hand rail should be attached. Some colleges have constructed cement ramps, and these have become so popular that nondisabled students use them regularly.

Underground passageways connecting two or more buildings can simplify the disabled student's entrances and exits to certain parts of the campus. In any college or university, certain buildings are more accessible than others. Occasionally, faculty members will agree to hold selected classes in these more accessible buildings in order to enable students in wheel chairs to attend.

Some educational institutions have their facilities centralized in a few buildings. An example of this is the "skyscraper" college or university housed in a tall building. This type of institution is especially attractive to students in wheel chairs because of its centralized character and the availability of elevators. However, this degree of centralization is uncommon. Any institution which is fairly compact and which has elevator service in its buildings may be suitable for students in wheel chairs. On extensive campuses, with student activities widely distributed, the disabled student tends to present more problems.

Even the most extensive of campuses may be suitable for some students who use wheel chairs. A number of these students have learned to drive, and, through special training, have mastered the techniques of entering and leaving their own cars. When assisted by special driving equipment, they have been found to be safe drivers, capable of dealing with almost all motoring problems. Such students move freely from one section of the campus to another. Often their paramount problem is parking. If a college lacks adequate parking facilities, special measures may be needed. One solution has been the reservation of parking spaces for handicapped students; another has been the opening of faculty facilities to them. In this connection, resistance is met only on the most crowded campuses where the faculties are most adamant. Some method is usually found for handling the cars of severely disabled students—those in wheel chairs or otherwise markedly limited in physical capacities. Special bus transportation for severely limited students is provided on a small number of college campuses.

Wheel chairs do not constitute much of a problem once the student has entered the classroom. It is customary for students to place their chairs in a corner of the room or in place of one of the regular classroom seats which has been moved aside. Frequently, the student carries a lap board with him which serves as a writing and study surface. Textbooks are carried in the lap or in a bag attached to the chair. Many students in wheel chairs can reach the blackboard and participate in board exercises. In addition, they are quite mobile in the classroom, moving easily from one part of the room to the other. In most respects, they require no additional attention from the instructor.

Consideration should be given to the location of certain facilities for the wheel-chair student. For example, his locker should be reasonably close to his classrooms and accessible with a minimum of aid or with no aid at all. If he lives on campus, his dormitory room should be centrally located and easily accessible. If the student lives off campus, the possibility of purchasing two sets of textbooks should be considered so that he may have fewer books to carry to and from the classroom and library study rooms.

If the student has limitations in shoulders, arms, and/or hands which restrict his ability to wheel his own chair, a number of possibilities may be tried. Volunteers may be used on a regular basis to assist the student or, if financially possible, he may hire a paid attendant. Each of these alternatives presents problems. A small number of students use wheel chairs with a small motor attached which enables it to move at a governed speed from one location to another. The student steers the chair with a lever designed to be managed by a person with even quite limited manipulative ability. These chairs move so deliberately that they do not constitute traffic or safety hazards on the campus. Through their use, some multiple-handicapped wheel-chair students are enabled to function more or less independently on the campus.

Adequate bathroom facilities are essential for the wheel-chair student. In most cases, existing facilities are satisfactory. However, facilities all over the campus should be surveyed to ascertain which are and are not suitable. The difficulty sometimes lies in the width of the entrance into the room itself as well as into the booths which contain the facilities. If entrances are too narrow, the custodial personnel can often suggest solutions which are neither costly nor time-consuming. The rehanging of a particular door or the replacement with draw curtains of the door on one of the booths may solve the problem. Sometimes the mere installation of a "grab rail" can be of inestimable assistance in facilitating the transfer from the chair to the facilities. Most students in wheel chairs have received rehabilitation training in working with such problems. A college or university interested in serving students in wheel chairs can benefit from the suggestions of rehabilitation personnel, many of whom participate daily in training persons in wheel chairs to perform activities of daily living successfully.

At first glance, it may seem that the accommodation of wheel-chair students represents a considerable problem. In many cases it does. Some institutions have not felt ready to make whatever adjustments might be needed. Those which have, however, have found that a little ingenuity and engineering go a long way. After the initial adaptations have been made, the student in the wheel chair functions independently. As time goes by, he becomes integrated into the academic and social life of the campus, requiring no more service than any other student. Some colleges and universities have found that expected problems failed to develop. Although the difficulties are real, the wheel-chair student and the community are almost always prepared to do more than their share to reduce the problem to manageable size.

THE STUDENT USING CRUTCHES OR CANES

Many of the problems of the wheel-chair student parallel those of students who use canes or crutches. Individuals using these aids have varying degrees of mobility and use different gaits. Some individuals using two crutches mount and descend steps with ease, have no difficulty in getting from one end of the campus to the other, and enter freely into almost all types of campus activity. Others are quite limited. The same observation holds true for those who use canes. The differences between people can be so sharp that generalizations made relative to one will be inapplicable to others. However, it should be noted that some of the members of this group benefit from compact campuses, elevators, and automobiles. The problems indicated for each of these in the section on wheel chairs have relevance here, too. However, one or two additional factors may be mentioned at this point.

The student on crutches or canes is usually self-sufficient. He will probably have little difficulty with bathroom facilities, but may be aided by a "grab rail" if it is installed. The person on crutches who has no manipulative limitations can manage most academic and social activities. In the classroom, he places his crutches unobtrusively, takes his seat, and meets all the physical requirements of classroom attendance. When class is over, he moves out with the other students, requiring virtually no special consideration. Occasionally, when a student has one activity following immediately upon another, he may require early dismissal from the first activity and/or late privileges in reporting to the second if his mobility is slow.

Slippery floors will mean that the student who uses crutches or canes must exercise more than ordinary caution. In most cases, this is not a problem. However, if the institution waxes some of its floors, these students should be informed of the fact. Crutches and canes usually have rubber or composition tips which provide adequate protection. If laboratory, bathroom, or other floors become wet and slippery, students should be asked to use special precautions or to wait until they have dried. Sometimes, nondisabled students may run into or trip over crutches or canes. In most cases, the disabled person is alert to the situation and avoids or minimizes the possibility of accident. By and large, canes and crutches are not important safety hazards in a college community.

THE STUDENT WITH LIMITED MANIPULATIVE ABILITY

A number of conditions may cause limitations in the use of the shoulders, arms, hands, and fingers. Among these are arthritis, amputations, accidents, poliomyelitis, cerebral palsy, disorders of the nervous system, and strokes. Severe limitations may interfere with such activities as writing, typing, carrying books, handling equipment in the laboratory, note-taking, and self-care. In manipulation, as in other types of limitations, the range of disability is broad. Furthermore, the degree of assistance which a person has received from rehabilitation services is often a key to the use he makes of his residual capacities. Limitations in the use of arms, hands, and shoulders may create focal problems for a college student and the institution which accepts him for matriculation. However, a few considerations may be helpful to such students.

If the fine movements required in handwriting are beyond the student's capacity, note-taking may be difficult for him. Some students ask others to make a duplicate set of notes for them. Others use the original notes made by other students for review and study. As indicated in the section dealing with blind students, this procedure has disadvantages. Yet for the student who cannot take any kind of notes for himself, the disadvantages seem small when measured against the prospect of having no notes at all or leaving college. Instructors may have to relax their usual insistence that each student take his own notes. If this is done and if a capable nondisabled student makes his notes or duplicates of them available to the disabled student, the barrier need not be an important one.

Most courses require themes, papers, reports, and other written evidences of work. The manually handicapped student who finds the fine finger movements required in handwriting impossible may be able to make the motions required in typing. If the standard typewriter fails to solve the problem, the electric typewriter is sometimes successful. Dictation is the final recourse for those students who cannot manage any form of typewriter. They record their materials on electronic tape or on a dictating machine, and the typist transcribes it, word for word. In some instances, the student will dictate directly to the typist, but this is feasible only if a skilled typist can be found. Some instructors accept the recorded materials, playing them back to evaluate the contents.

The loss of one hand need not be a barrier to written communication. When the writing hand has been amputated, rehabilitation services will train an individual to write legibly with the remaining hand. Research in methods of one-handed typing has proved successful. The manually handicapped students can prepare neat manuscripts, using the Dvorak or comparable typing system, and with or without a specially designed keyboard. There are records of cases which are less usual—some double-arm amputees write legibly, holding the pencil with their mouths or toes; some individuals who have lost function in both hands use a typewriter whose keys are controlled by the breath of the individual. These examples indicate that a mere statement of physical losses does not automatically indicate the dimensions of the problem. Prior to deciding the collegiate future of a student, all possible avenues of assistance should be explored. Sometimes, imagination and engineering skill can overcome seemingly impassable barriers.

Manual limitations may be so extensive that it is impossible or unsafe to handle laboratory equipment. Some institutions "play it safe" by excluding most students with manual limitations from actual laboratory work wherever damage to equipment or persons is regarded as a possibility. Quite often, these judgments are made in a blanket fashion. A more individualized approach would assess the limitations of each individual and limit the exclusion to those areas which are prudently thought to constitute hazards for the student, his colleagues, and college property. Even if a student is excluded from actual participation in some or all of the laboratory activities in a course, there is often little reason to exclude him altogether from the laboratory. The types of learning that take place there are essential to student growth. And if the manually limited student is not permitted to be an active participant in the experiments, he can still learn much from observing other students. Many laboratories are conducted on a student team basis, with two or more students working together on the problems presented. In such cases, the disabled student can work with another student, performing some of the routine jobs wherever possible.

Manually limited students who cannot manage the activities of daily living present fairly serious problems to an institution. They may have difficulties in such life functions as washing, dressing, toilet habits, getting in and out of bed, chairs, and overclothes. They may not be fully independent in eating, requiring assistance and/or special eating utensils. Yet such students may be intellectually able, and may have contributions to make both to college life and to the postcollege world. Sometimes these students arrange for full- or part-time attendants to assist them. Such attendants may solve a major proportion of the student's physical adjustment problems, but the problem may arise of how these attendants should be integrated into the campus situation. Some institutions have adopted a policy of rejecting students who require the services of attendants. Others have felt that this is not a major adjustment and have been able to work with such students successfully. A college that is sincerely interested in providing education to severely disabled students may experiment with the use of attendants in a limited number of cases. Such experimentation may lead to the consummation of a successful experience for all concerned.

Use of the hands is so often perceived as essential to college work that it is sometimes difficult for educators to understand how it is possible for a student with severe manual limitations to function in college. Yet the records are rich with cases of such students who have achieved success in college and have gone on to important careers in many fields. Some of the success is due to the excellent rehabilitation services which the students received. Much of it is due to the attitudes of the colleges and universities which agreed to enroll them.

Some of the adjustments which institutions can make to assist disabled students have been briefly discussed. Many disabled students will need to have some of these adjustments; some will need only a few. As a matter of fact, the individuality of disabled students suggests that no list can be complete. The range of limitations is as unpredictable as the range of potential capacities. Each case should be studied separately and apart from all others. Adjustments that are helpful to some deaf students may be less helpful to others. Furthermore, such disability groups as cardiacs, epileptics, post-tubercular cases, and other systemic disorders have not been discussed. Even in these categories, individual students will have needs that must be considered in terms of the student's unique situation.

It is clear that some institutions have been more successful in accommodating severely disabled students than others. In some cases, this has been due to a unique physical plant, special interest of key personnel, pressures of the community, interest of the faculty, and institutional emphasis on service to the individual student. Perhaps the major barrier to this type of success in more institutions lies in the area of people's feelings. When an administration and a faculty have positive attitudes toward accepting and educating severely disabled students, ways are found to solve the mechanical problems. When an institution fails to develop a positive concept of itself as an educator of severely disabled youth, the tremendous resources of such youth, the community, and the institution itself fail to be mobilized for the purpose. Apparently the major variable is not a special type of campus, counseling service, or faculty, but a vigorous leadership committed to the principle that the function of the institution is to teach intellectually able students capable of benefiting from instruction.

The Admission of Physically Handicapped Students

3

COLLEGES AND UNIVERSITIES are relatively specific about their academic requirements for admission, and usually spell them out in terms of numbers of high school units, grades, and subjects. In the areas of health and character, specificity is less common. Personality traits and physical capacities are more difficult to quantify. They do not lend themselves to ready definition. Furthermore, beyond a general requirement of "good moral character" and "good health," there is a lack of agreement about desirable limits in these areas. As a result, most institutions function in a vague, gray area in setting and enforcing physical health standards for admission. Administrative officers, faculty, applicants for admission, and students are likely to be somewhat confused about the physical capacities required for admission. Under these circumstances, the tendency is to weigh every case without firm reference to a rational college policy.

Are admissions standards drawn in physical terms really necessary? Some professional educators believe that the regularly stated academic requirements suffice. A student's high school record, letters of reference, personal interviews, and admissions test scores are thought to be indicative of his potentialities for success in college work. Advocates of this position fail to realize that college attendance makes physical and emotional demands on an individual that are interwoven with the academic demands. A student's intellectual ability to master the content of a course is conditioned by his capacity to gain access to the classroom and library materials associated with the course. A student's facility in

English composition can be assessed only if he has the physical capacities to engage in written communication. A large number of similar examples could be offered. However, the evidence seems clear. Just as a minimum level of intellectual ability may be required to perform successfully in a particular institution, a comparable level of physical capacity may also be required to meet the demands of academic and social life on the campus.

This does not argue for special admissions standards for physically handicapped students. On the contrary, it indicates a need for more definitive admissions requirements for all students. At this time, most colleges and universities have such standards, but they lack definition and clarity. It is essential for the physically handicapped students, as for all students, that a set of rational requirements be constructed to guide participants in the admissions procedure in making adequate decisions. These requirements should apply to all students, physically handicapped or not. When this is done, an institution is more likely to admit students who can function effectively in its academic environment. Furthermore, an applicant is more likely to seek and gain admission to an institution in which his physical limitations will not serve as major barriers to learning.

The general requirements of such an admissions program should be based on the adoption of a policy governing physical standards. This policy should emanate from the top policy-making body of the college, serving as a reference point for more specific standards. A general policy adopted by one institution* is as follows:

1. The student's health status shall not constitute a danger to any individual or group. . . .
2. The health condition shall not be such that it may be aggravated or intensified by the demands of attendance at the College.
3. The limitations of activity required by any health problem shall be such that the program adjustments necessary will still enable the student to conform with academic college requirements.
4. The health status shall be such that the student may be expected to continue his college work with a reasonable number of hours on a continuing basis until its completion within a reasonable period of time.

* *Hunter College Bulletin.* School of General Studies, 1960, p. 24.

These generalized policy statements have functioned satisfactorily in this college situation. Individual institutions may wish to adapt them to meet local needs. Notwithstanding the wording and the degree of inclusiveness, the creation of a policy statement is an essential first step. Without it, college personnel will have difficulty in formulating logical approaches to the problem of admitting the severely handicapped student.

ESTABLISHING AN ADMISSIONS POLICY

Once a policy has been established, one or more committees are usually charged with the function of "spelling out" admissions requirements in physical terms. Participants in such committee work often include a physician, admissions officers, representatives of the dean of students and the faculty, and guidance personnel. Prior to setting up an admissions structure relating to physical capacities, these committees generally consider certain essential elements in their own institution which seem to bear on the problem. The points discussed below indicate the range of factors which may need to be weighed.

General Philosophy of the Institution

Some colleges and universities are less guidance-oriented than others. Such institutions have established a framework of student functioning which is believed to be in accordance with the minimum requirements of attendance in that institution. Student performance at levels below these expectations are viewed with concern. If a student fails to "measure up," it may be decided that he lacks the qualities essential to continued participation in the college community. After a reasonable period during which the student is expected to raise the level of his performance, he may be dropped if he fails to do so.

On the other hand, some institutions provide students with extensive guidance resources. They are concerned not only with the facts of failure, but also with the dynamics. Using the faculty and supportive professional counseling personnel, such institutions assist the student to gain self-understanding and to work with college officials toward ascertaining the desirability of remaining in the institution.

This comparison represents only one dimension of college philosophy. Others are reflected in the comparative rigidity of the curriculum and the academic demands made on the student, the degree of individual instruction and guidance favored by the institution, and the relationships established between faculty and students. Each institution, although individual in its approach, may be placed on a continuum of concern for the individual student and readiness to offer him individualized teaching and personnel services. A committee setting limits for the admission of physically handicapped students should be aware of the place of the institution on this continuum. Institutions which are "tough-minded" and offer relatively few services of a supportive nature are likely to be less feasible for severely physically handicapped students. If this is the case, the admissions personnel should apply standards which tend to make the institution relatively exclusive, in so far as severely disabled students are concerned. In reality, such students require more individualized guidance. However, if the philosophy of the college places stress on individual differences and adapts itself readily to such differences, it may be able to work more successfully with severely disabled students.

Attitudinal and Emotional Climate of the Institution

There are institutions which have a traditional interest in the physically handicapped. Some of these have been serving such students for long periods of time; in others, key administrators and/or faculty members have given leadership to institutional attitudes toward disabled students. As a matter of fact, some colleges and universities have developed pride in this service and regard it as a major educational contribution. A few instances have been noted of institutions which have not only accepted severely disabled students, but have made an effort to attract them.

On the other hand, some colleges and universities, despite a diversity of feeling among administrators and faculty members, are less hospitable to the idea of educating severely handicapped students. Often, the tone is set by the leadership. Such institutions are inclined to undertake services to the disabled student with great caution. They tend to emphasize considerations of safety, faculty time required, and the inadequacy of physical and instructional resources. In this type of institution, admission requirements may

be restrictive, if stated at all. In most cases they are not formalized, but the disabled students and their advisers sense an atmosphere of less than wholehearted acceptance.

Most institutions fall between the extremes of actively recruit-
ing and overtly rejecting physically handicapped students. Committees working with the problem of admitting disabled students
tend to be composed of individuals who, in part, reflect the institutional atmosphere. Consequently, they will introduce this consideration into committee deliberations.

Legal Factors Involved

Legal considerations may enter into admissions decisions relating to handicapped college students. Institutions are often concerned lest the admission of such students impose legal responsibilities in excess of those relating to other students. They may
consider such issues as insurance costs, liability for injury, and
responsibility to nondisabled students who may become involved
in accidents in which disabled persons are participants. Each institution should explore the legal implications with its legal consultants. By and large, the evidence is that, in accepting severely
disabled students, colleges and universities do not generally take
on additional legal obligations, but this is often conditioned by the
provision that reasonable precautions must be exercised. The precise nature of these precautions has not been legally tested, but the
opinion has been expressed that normal procedures employed in
most colleges and universities could be construed as constituting
prudent management.

It should be recognized, however, that a number of points in
this area have not been fully clarified. For example, a member of
a science department raised the question of a disabled student
working in a laboratory. If, as a result of his own behavior or that
of others, the disabled student should be injured, it appears that
there would be no special liability. However, assuming that such
a student has an accident which results in injury to a nondisabled
student, could the nondisabled student hold the college responsible
for admitting a handicapped student to the laboratory? Consulta-
tions with lawyers and rehabilitation personnel have not succeeded
in clarifying the responsibility of the institution.

Obviously, questions of safety and legal liability must be carefully considered in formulating admissions policies and procedures. Municipal and state colleges may be confronted by another legal problem in relation to admissions. Under the law, such institutions may be directed to admit students meeting specified qualifications. Often, these are stated in terms of residence, academic achievement, and personal character. Rarely are physical factors incorporated into such legislation. The question has therefore been raised: "May a publicly supported institution deny admission to a student who meets all the legal qualifications, but who is considered by the duly constituted admissions committees to lack the physical capacity for attendance?" Apparently, legal clarification on this point is yet to be achieved. In one large municipal college system, legal counsel has ruled that admission may be denied to students who, after careful consideration, are found to be physically unsuited to the institution. However, this opinion represents a finding in relation to only one institution and has not been tested in the courts.

Relationships with Rehabilitation Services

A substantial part of the rehabilitation service offered in the United States is administered by rehabilitation agencies which are part of state departments of education and social welfare. In New York State, for example, rehabilitation services are administered at the level of an Assistant Commissioner of Education and a Commission for the Blind. Public institutions are likely to be part of, or closely related to, the state department of education. Where this relationship is close, the total educational effort of the state may require cooperative interaction between rehabilitation agencies and state and municipal colleges and universities. These relationships may be of such a nature that the public institution is expected to serve students referred by the rehabilitation agencies, whenever possible. In some instances, similar pressures exist for privately supported schools. Indirectly, this pressure may be expressed for smaller institutions through student recruitment and fees. Colleges and universities with favorable attitudes toward disabled students are likely to be more widely used as sources of education and training by state rehabilitation agencies. When such students are admitted to a private college or university, the state rehabilitation agency will often pay all fees, including certain extraordinary costs for such services as tutoring and reading, and for special equipment such as typewriters and recording equipment.

Number of Severely Handicapped Students to Be Admitted

Some institutions maintain a type of quota system. For example, one institution has considered setting limits on the number of wheel-chair cases that can be admitted. This is based on the already heavy demands made on the elevator services in its buildings. Another institution has informally placed limits on the number of blind students it will accept, basing its decision on the belief that such students require extra instructorial and clerical time while the limited resources of the institution can absorb only that degree of extra work represented by its stated quota. A third institution has restricted the number of students on crutches that it will accommodate at any one time. This restriction grows out of the feeling that students on crutches represent dangers to themselves and others during the busy period when students are changing classes. It has been thought that more than a stated number of such students would constitute an inordinate safety hazard.

Admissions committees tend to consider the numbers of severely disabled students whom they can serve effectively. They rarely arrive at a definite quota, but some type of limitation is often implicit in their decisions. Frequently such decisions come into being without direct consultation with specialists in the education and rehabilitation of the physically handicapped.

Limits on the Types and Degrees of Disability to Be Admitted

In their considerations, some admissions committees look more favorably on the admission of persons with certain types of disabilities. One large municipal college has had extensive and successful experience in serving blind and hearing handicapped students but it has established a rationale which excludes applicants with severe restrictions in mobility. In the same community, one college is highly restrictive in admitting students with epilepsy; another is much less so. One large university will accept most disabilities, but will be exceedingly hesitant about admitting a speech handicapped applicant. Limitations regarding types of disabling conditions are also manifested in admission to various curricula in a single institution. One department or curriculum may admit persons with severe cardiac problems. Another, with roughly the same demands on the student, may not. Each will be able to indicate its rationale for its position. By and large, these rationales reflect feelings more than tested experiences with handicapped students.

Another admissions problem is based on the degree of disability. Thus, within a particular diagnostic category, the less disabled applicants may gain admission, while the more disabled may not. An institution may admit visually handicapped students who are legally blind but have partial vision while it excludes certain students who are totally blind. Yet the evidence would indicate that the degree of vision is not the crucial factor. The important variable is the total functioning of the individual. In reality, some totally blind students require less assistance than do some partially seeing ones. Arbitrary limitations on admission based on degrees of severity are likely to ignore the individual capacities of some persons to work effectively despite very severe disablements.

Academic Ability Required

Some admissions groups reason that a disability erects barriers which require superior ability if the student is to overcome them. They react more positively to severely disabled students who present evidence of superior intellectual and academic ability. Thus, they many stipulate, as one institution does, that blind persons will be admitted if they meet academic standards in excess of those demanded of other students. In many cases, this consideration is less explicit. However, more than one admissions committee functions in a way to suggest that some cases are decided on the basis of demonstrated academic ability above and beyond that required of all other students.

One reason offered for this approach is that the college has to give more to the disabled student. Since its resources are usually limited, the institution should not require its staff to overextend itself on behalf of disabled persons who barely meet the regular admissions standards. This reasoning has a superficial validity. It appeals to some faculty members who are likely to accept the basic premise, namely, that students with higher initial ability are likely to perform more successfully. Experience with disabled students suggests that variables other than intellectual ability and academic achievement play a role in college success. Given the essential minimum of ability required by the institution, other factors may come into play. For example, some disabled students who have been able to adapt to severe disability and to profit from rehabilitation service may have difficulties in the college environment despite exceptional ability and academic achievement. Often, less gifted students, highly motivated by a need to compensate for their limitations, may attain superior levels of college achievement through consistent application and determined effort.

A number of factors have been discussed which are frequently considered by admissions groups in implementing college policy and admitting individual physically disabled students. Some or all of them may be highly significant in a particular institution. If so, they should form a framework for admissions decisions. However, they constitute a background rather than a figure. The central focus is a more rational and universal one. It is a consideration which supersedes all others and should take precedence in admissions decisions.

PHYSICAL DEMANDS AND STUDENT CAPACITIES

One approach to the admissions problems of physically handicapped students draws on job-analysis techniques which have proved successful in industry. In a typical college or university, staff members with special competence in this area may be used as consultants. Such personnel may include engineers, business management specialists, personnel workers, and vocational guidance counselors. In the absence of competent faculty in this area, a college administration may consult with local state and private rehabilitation agencies. These agencies will often cooperate in making a survey of study demands. The survey itself usually encompasses five steps.

1. General College Environment

Every college has a physical plant which is unique in certain respects. Physical features which require assessment are the number and height of steps on the campus, availability of ramps, possibilities of gaining access to key buildings from ground level, presence of elevators, extensiveness of the campus, accessibility of parking space for handicapped drivers, acoustics in lecture rooms, effectiveness of lighting in classrooms and offices, width of doorways, ease of entrance into and use of bathroom facilities, slipperiness of floors and stairs, availability of suitable rooms for reading and tutoring, and others.

Assisted by consultants, the admissions committee should make a full survey of the college plant, and each feature should be studied in terms of the student capacities which it demands. Both the physical demands and student capacities should be systematically recorded and organized. Wherever possible, a specialist in special education and/or rehabilitation should participate in the survey. His understandings and insights may sharpen the process and add to its scientific precision. If necessary, disabled volunteers may be asked to try out various facilities and report their reactions. In one college, for example, applicants in wheel chairs were escorted around the building to ascertain the suitability of the environment for their needs.

2. Academic Functioning

College-level academic work requires such basic physical faculties as ability to see, to hear, to manipulate, to ambulate, to speak, to write, to perceive, and to respond appropriately. To illustrate, participation in a college laboratory course in chemistry requires ability to use arms, shoulders, hands, and fingers to manipulate apparatus and substances safely and effectively. A course in art appreciation demands minimum levels of visual acuity. A course in music appreciation demands some degree of hearing. A field course in geology makes ambulation a necessity, while a course in conversational French requires a certain level of speech ability. The number of examples could be extended manyfold. The essential fact is that each curriculum area should be analyzed realistically in terms of the requirements which it makes on students.

If organized solely by faculty members, such a survey will be conducted with inadequate regard for professional job-analysis considerations. In such cases the data derived may be subjective and incomplete. Experience reveals that some faculty members minimize the demands in their subject areas, and as a result, students are admitted to essential courses which make greater demands on them than they had expected. On the other hand, faculty members who exaggerate the levels of physical functioning required in their courses eliminate qualified students.

One technique used to level off these sources of error is to employ outside consultants with special skills in job analysis. An analysis emanating from a group advised by such "experts" may reduce excessive optimism and pessimism regarding severely disabled students. A science instructor insisted that he could not accommodate students using crutches in his laboratory sections. He believed that such students had to rely on their crutches for balance and support, and thus were more susceptible to laboratory accidents. A dispassionate study of the laboratory functions revealed that well-trained crutch users were as free of accident hazards as other students. A physiology instructor believed that touching models of the human body would be equivalent to seeing them for a blind student. Although much can be learned in such a situation through the use of touch, it is not an adequate substitute for visual perception in this instance.

College instructors tend to bring their feelings about handicapped students into the classroom. These attitudes influence their concepts of how well disabled students can function in their courses. Often, they will not be aware of such attitudes or they will deny them for a variety of reasons. Somehow, a way must be discovered to reduce the effects of preconceptions. The technique found most helpful is to have a survey made by a faculty committee assisted by an acknowledged expert in job-analysis techniques. Admittedly, the results of an objective evaluation of this type may be challenged by some faculty members with strong feelings. Yet the findings will serve as a base for further college action in defining admissions standards, even though not all of them can be adopted immediately if there is internal resistance.

3. Appraisal of Physical Capacities of Applicants

At the conclusion of the second step, the college should be in possession of a catalogue of the minimum physical demands which its environment makes on all students, as well as on those who major and minor in certain curriculum areas. These demands will often be expressed in terms of the required levels of seeing, hearing, manipulating, speaking, ambulating, writing, perceiving, and responding. If at all possible, each area will be described in quantitative and/or descriptive terms and will serve as a yardstick for admissions procedures.

Each disabled applicant should be exposed to a standardized appraisal process. Using the same areas and terms employed in setting up the academic demands of college study, college officers, assisted at times by community consultants, should make a detailed analysis of the physical capacities of each applicant. A careful evaluation should be prepared of vision, hearing, manipulative ability, speech, handwriting, mobility, perceptual abilities, and means of response. This may be accomplished through the combined efforts of physicians, psychologists, counselors, and community rehabilitation workers. When completed, it should be in the form of a systematic survey, using the same frame of reference that is used in analyzing academic demands. Frequently the forms used for both operations will be similar.

4. Matching Process

At this point, the admissions officers should have two comparable sets of physical analysis data available—a statement of the physical demands of attendance in the institution and a statement of the physical capacities of the applicant. Since both are couched in the same terms and fit into the same context, it is possible to match them. As the student's capacities are measured, item by item, against the demands of college attendance, a pattern will emerge: The student may be physically competent to engage in all college activities, many college activities, some college activities, or very few.

A picture of how the student measures up physically to what the college expects of him is now available for study by both the student and the faculty and administration. If an institution demanded that every student meet its physical requirements fully, very few applicants would be admitted. In a society in which few individuals are physically capable in all areas of human functioning, the imperfect human being is more common than his perfect counterpart.

5. Adapting Physical Demands to Student Capacities

Many applicants for admission will fail to meet all the physical requirements established by the institution in the four steps above.

In some cases, this failure will be considered meaningful in every aspect of the student's program. For example, a deaf student may lack the lip-reading ability necessary to follow connected discourse in the classroom. A blind student may lack Braille techniques and typing ability to take notes and prepare papers. An orthopedically handicapped student may be unable to get from one class to the next without assistance, and this may not be available. When these limitations are major and meaningful, the college may decide that they extend beyond the level at which effective education may take place.

On the other hand, the typical physically handicapped applicant often fails to meet standards in ways which are less significant. A student may lack dexterity to participate in laboratory courses, but he may be able to keep his own notes and write his own examinations. A student in a wheel chair may not be able to attend classes on the second floor of buildings, but may function quite adequately within a schedule which is limited to first-floor classes. A blind student may be unable to see blackboard work which is so important in most mathematics instruction, but with the help of tutoring and special consideration from the instructor, he may be able to manage some courses in this area.

Each institution must arrive at its own decisions as to which physical capacity requirements must be rigidly enforced and which can be waived or modified. Many disabled students use substitute techniques for meeting academic problems. The blind student may rely on electronic recording of required readings. The deaf student may profit from individual tutoring by a classmate or a senior student. The student with real manipulation problems may gain substantially from watching other students perform required laboratory experiments. The student who is unable to write or type may dictate his work to another person.

It is in the fifth step that the college or university comes to grips with the problem of its own standards and how far it is prepared to modify them to meet individual needs. Some institutions have moved boldly in the direction of permitting disabled students to function in a variety of idiosyncratic ways. Others have not. The evidence compiled by the former group tends to support the belief that many modifications may be permitted without "watering down" the curriculum and without surrendering high academic levels of achievement. Students with very severe limitations, functioning in a sympathetic and realistic college atmosphere, have achieved outstanding records. A rigid interpretation of physical standards might have excluded them from a college experience.

There is no formula which applies to all colleges and universities. All that is available is evidence that the willingness to work with severely handicapped young people and the community often results in a successful experience for all participants. The fact that service to physically disabled applicants cannot be reduced to a formula argues for the college use of student personnel services. These services may adequately evaluate such students and cultivate an open-minded attitude toward sifting the essential from the incidental in statements of physical demands of college attendance.

An example of a guide developed by one institution is presented in the pages following. Such a guide may not be suitable for other colleges and universities. However, it has functioned satisfactorily in this one setting and may suggest ideas that can be used in other institutions.

SOME COMPONENTS OF AN ADMISSIONS POLICY

In formulating its admissions policy, the individual college or university may wish to include a number of areas which are relevant to the admission of physically handicapped students. Among these are:

Admissions Requirements for All Students

A statement of the admissions requirements that apply generally conveys to the disabled applicant and the community that all students are perceived as fundamentally alike and subject to the same regulations. Furthermore, if the disabled student appreciates from the beginning that he is not viewed as an exception or as an extraordinary case, it tends to ease his ultimate assimilation into the college community. Special educators and rehabilitation workers are firm in the belief that integration into nondisabled groups is desirable for most physically handicapped college students. This is borne out by the fact that, with the exception of Gallaudet College in Washington, D.C., which serves deaf students exclusively,

Name......................   *Date*..........

FUNCTIONAL ANALYSIS FOR PHYSICALLY HANDICAPPED STUDENTS

SEEING

Capable of doing own reading?
Capable of reading blackboard?
Capable of seeing demonstrations?
Capable of viewing films?
Capable of viewing pictures?
Capable of sighted travel through building?
Capable of doing own diagrams?
Special adjustments required:
....Lighting
....Lenses
....Readers
....Guides
....Oral instruction
....Talking book
....Braille
....Large typewriter
....Heavy dark pencil
....Special orientation to building and classes
....Other adjustments
Recommendation for visual evaluation?
Comments and recommendations.

Interviewer.......................

Name........................   Date..........

FUNCTIONAL ANALYSIS FOR PHYSICALLY HANDICAPPED STUDENTS

HEARING

Normal interview conversation?
In a large classroom?
Normal range of radio or tape recorder?
Interference from normal traffic noises and other extraneous sounds?
Functional use of hearing aid?
Attitude toward hearing aid?
Lip reading?
Special adjustments:
....Seat in front of room
....Louder presentation by instructor
....More careful articulation by instructor
....More board illustration and written materials
....Special hearing devices
Referral to Speech and Hearing Clinic for evaluation?
Comments and recommendations.

Interviewer........................

———————————————

Name........................   Date..........

FUNCTIONAL ANALYSIS FOR PHYSICALLY HANDICAPPED STUDENTS

WRITING

Capable of writing classroom notes?
Resources for dictating notes.
Knowledge of typing.
Capable of writing on blackboard?
Special adjustments required.
Comments and recommendations.

Interviewer........................

———————————————

Name......................   *Date*..........

FUNCTIONAL ANALYSIS FOR PHYSICALLY HANDICAPPED STUDENTS

SPEECH

Interview impressions:
  Clarity
  Rapidity
  Accent
  Loudness
Ease of verbal communication.
Adequate for classroom use?
Adequate for speech courses?
Adequate for occupational choice?
Recommendation for evaluation by Speech and Hearing Clinic.
Comments and recommendations.

Interviewer.......................

Name......................   *Date*..........

FUNCTIONAL ANALYSIS FOR PHYSICALLY HANDICAPPED STUDENTS

SPECIAL HEALTH PROBLEMS

Description of condition.
Special medication and health care required.
Activity limitations.
Possible curriculum limitations.
Progressive or static.
Special adjustments needed.
Referral for evaluation to Rehabilitation Center?
Comments and recommendations.

Interviewer.......................

Name........................   *Date*..........

FUNCTIONAL ANALYSIS FOR PHYSICALLY HANDICAPPED STUDENTS

MANIPULATION

Capable of self-care in building?
Capable of handling laboratory equipment safely?
Capable of writing using pen and pencil?
Capable of handling chalk in classroom?
Capable of eating by self-feeding?
Capable of carrying own books?
Capable of turning pages?
Capable of handling coins?
Capable of steady hand movements?
Capable of speedy hand movements?
Capable of two-handed coordinated movements?
Capable of picking up gross objects?
Capable of picking up fine objects?
Capable of opening doors?
Capable of typing movements?
Capable of raising hand for instructor's attention?
Capable of manipulating papers?
Others.
Adjustments required?
Referral to Rehabilitation Center for evaluation?
Comments and recommendations.

Interviewer........................

Name........................   Date..........

FUNCTIONAL ANALYSIS FOR PHYSICALLY HANDICAPPED STUDENTS

MOBILITY

Travel to and from college.
Travel on level surfaces.
Special devices used.
Walking up and down steps.
Relative speed of mobility.
Steadiness and balance.
Assistance required.
Ability to sit in and rise from chair.
Ability to walk up incline.
Ability to walk on hard smooth surface.
Ability to pass through narrow aisles and doorways.
Special aids required:
....Special elevator service
....Early dismissal
....Student helper
....Elimination of field trips
....Paid attendant
....Close safety supervision
....Others
Referral to Rehabilitation Center for evaluation?
Comments and recommendations.

Interviewer........................

specialized collegiate institutions for the physically disabled have never taken firm root in this country. Integration is hastened by the establishment of common standards for all, even though some handicapped students may need special tools and opportunities to conform to these standards.

Self-care

The disabled student should have received education and rehabilitation services which permit him to function as a relatively independent person in the college setting. The institution should not be responsible for providing special supervisory care relating to the activities of daily living. Thus, the applicant should provide evidence that he is capable of washing, dressing, caring for toilet needs, maintaining his belongings in orderly fashion, and fulfilling the normal requirements of personal appearance and demeanor.

The college does not have the functions or the resources of the rehabilitation center and may properly demand a minimum level of self-care from every applicant for admission. In assessing self-care capabilities of a severely handicapped student, an institution can use the facilities of a hospital, rehabilitation center, or community agency. This assessment is best performed by specialists such as physicians, physical and occupational therapists, and rehabilitation counselors. If a student is found deficient in self-care activities, remedial work may be suggested and the student may apply for admission at a later date. Most physically limited applicants who have not already received rehabilitation services can benefit from such programs and achieve adequate self-care.

Reading, Study Habits, and Note-taking

A number of colleges and universities offer noncredit courses in study habits and reading skills. These courses are part of an attempt to work with students who apparently lack some of the basic tools necessary for college-level study. It has been suggested that the exclusion of students with inadequate reading skills and study habits would drastically reduce the college population. Although disabled students should be subject to the same admissions standards in reading and note-taking as other students, any deficiencies may be especially handicapping to a student with sensory, perceptual, and manipulative limitations. For this reason the institution should ascertain each applicant's current level of functioning in the basic learning tools.

Some disabled students have been educated at home, in special schools, and in modified classes. In such educational settings, special provisions are usually made for reading, note-taking, and study skills. In a college-level institution, special provisions of this type are less common. In the first place, college study makes heavier demands on reading speed and accuracy than high school work. The casual note-taking which may have sufficed in secondary school is not adequate for college study. And while a poorly organized study schedule may not have constituted a major barrier in high school, it is often conducive to failure in college. Second, colleges are structured for all students. Few institutions can provide the adjustments offered by special schools and classes in public and private elementary and secondary schools. Consequently, the physically handicapped student should demonstrate proficiency in reading, study habits, and note-taking.

Some physical disabilities have obvious effects on these skills. For example, a blind student should be required to offer proof that his mastery of Braille is adequate for taking notes, that he has the resources for managing a heavy reading load, and that, with assistance, he can function in a library. Individuals with manual limitations should be asked to show that they have some method of taking notes. Deaf persons who learned language without the use of hearing are often limited in this area and should be assessed in terms of their ability to understand college-level abstract concepts and vocabularies. Individuals who have health problems which lead to frequent absences should be asked to indicate their plans for keeping up to date in their work and maintaining a satisfactory level of achievement.

It would be desirable for most colleges and universities to set minimum standards of reading, note-taking, and study habits for all students. In many cases, such standards are implicit and loosely enforced. Even though physically disabled students should not be excluded for causes not applicable to other students, the college can reasonably expect them to undertake remedial work in needed areas.

Demands on Instructional Staff

Some institutions have teaching situations which make heavy demands on the nonclassroom time of instructors. Along with teaching responsibilities, members of the staff may have heavy committee assignments, administrative work, supervision of field workers and student teachers, research commitments, community activities, extension work, and the like. In such instances, the college or university should be concerned with the additional demands which physically disabled students may make on staff time and energy. It should be recognized that few physically disabled applicants will make heavy demands. On the other hand, a strong student personnel service may reduce the instructor's load in working with such students.

Despite ancillary services, however, it should be expected that the presence of a severely disabled student in a class will necessitate some additional service from the instructor. This service may be in the form of verbally explaining board illustrations to a blind student, speaking more slowly and clearly for a hearing handicapped student, or giving a stutterer sufficient time and opportunity to express himself even if this causes some tension on the part of the teacher. The number of variations of types of additional service which may be asked of an instructor is great. In considering admissions policies, a college may have to take a stand in terms of how much it is willing to ask of its teaching staff. On almost every faculty there is likely to be one or more teachers who feel negatively about such extra services. Often, in admitting a student with a severe disability, an institution may be confronted by the need to avoid assigning this student to certain faculty members. At times, instructors willing to be assigned such students find themselves penalized in having to assume not only their own responsibilities, but those of some of their colleagues as well.

Vocational Goal of the Disabled Student

Colleges and universities do not always perceive the function of the undergraduate school in vocational terms. Usually the emphasis is on liberal arts, directed toward enriching the total life of the student and providing him with the ability to think critically about his environment. It is exceedingly rare that a college takes the applicant's vocational goal into account in considering him for entrance into an undergraduate liberal arts program. It is assumed that the very act of learning in a college atmosphere will assist a student to make vocational choices and to prepare for them. However, whether or not a student has a realistic vocation in mind seems hardly relevant to the admitting institution.

Among disabled students, on the other hand, the vocational goal may take on a significant role in his college education. Under current federal and state legislation, some college students with severe disablements receive financial aid from their state rehabilitation agencies. Such aid may include tuition, books, supplies, and other related expenses, and is administered in the legal framework of *vocational* rehabilitation. Thus, before a prospective college student can be assured of continuing assistance under this legislation, he must arrive at a vocational goal which is considered by the rehabilitation service to be reasonable and achievable. Therefore, the need to choose a vocation is a reality to many disabled college students. In considering applicants who may need assistance in making such a choice, the college should take into account the present level of career planning and the availability of state rehabilitation services in the light of such planning. Applicants who need financial aid from rehabilitation sources but have not yet made firm occupational choices may be considered differently from others who are actively sponsored by the state rehabilitation agencies and have made realistic choices.

ADMISSIONS PROCEDURES FOR PHYSICALLY HANDICAPPED APPLICANTS

Admissions procedures for disabled students usually involve three college services: the medical office, the counseling office, the admissions office and the admissions committee.

The Medical Office

In working with physically handicapped applicants for admission, the institution relies heavily on the college medical office, using the physician in various ways. Some require every applicant, disabled or not, to undergo a physical examination at the college. Such examinations may include X rays, blood tests, urinalyses, sedimentation rates, etc. In some situations, large groups of applicants or entering students appear at an examining center where they are examined by a battery of physicians, moving in assembly-line fashion similar to World War II draftees. In other cases, the student may make an appointment for a private examination by the college physician who will gather data essential for admissions decisions.

Many large institutions face the imposing problem of screening thousands of applicants during a few months each spring. Some of these colleges waive the pre-admission physical examination. In its place, the college may plan an examination *after* the student is admitted, or it may rely on the health report submitted by the student's own physician. Each of these methods has its advantages and disadvantages. The college physician and the administration must make joint decisions concerning the type and extent of physical examination which provides the most complete data in the most practical ways.

Naturally, the conduct of the examination lies within the professional judgment of the physician. Ordinarily, the institution raises questions and looks to the doctor for answers. On many occasions, the physician may not be able to ascertain the precise data and offer the specific answers desired. In any event, the primary role of the doctor is fact finding. Typically, the physician does not serve as a substitute for an admissions office or committee, but rather submits the raw materials for their decisions. Among the questions medical personnel are asked to answer are:

1.   Will college attendance constitute a danger to this applicant or to others in the college community?

2.   Does this applicant have a physical condition which renders him susceptible to further tissue damage as a result of participating in one or more required college activities?

3.   Does the applicant have the physical capacity to cope with the academic and social demands of college life?

4.   Will the applicant's condition prevent him from carrying a normal program which he can complete within a reasonable period of time?

In addition to data relating to these four questions, the college physician is chiefly responsible for "spelling out" the physical capacities of the applicant in the same terms as the college uses to indicate the physical demands of college attendance. This is often done on a rating scale which lists such abilities as walking, climbing, running, standing, crawling, seeing, hearing, maintaining balance, and so on. These rating scales often present a challenge to the college physician for most doctors are not trained to view individuals in terms of physical capacities and are more comfortable with concepts of pathology, etiology, and treatment. Furthermore, some physicians believe that such estimates are too gross and communicate little to the student and the administration.

These beliefs are less often held by physicians in industry and by specialists in physical medicine and rehabilitation. As a result, the physician with such a background or with special training in these areas has much to contribute to college admissions procedures. Naturally, the personality and interests of the individual physician play an important role in determining how he functions with disabled students. The situation is often helped when the college has some connection with a hospital or a rehabilitation center or both. If the facilities of either or both can be made available, the admissions program is likely to be more scientific and discerning.

Since the physician in a college setting serves, in part, as a gatherer of data for administrative personnel, he must be able to communicate readily with lay persons. He must be prepared to interpret findings in simple terms to individuals with limited insights into the anatomy and physiology of the human body and with restricted medical vocabularies. Often, the physician has to function as an educator, defining terms, explaining disease entities, and answering naïve questions.

Frequently, the physician has to gather vital data from other medical sources such as family physicians, hospitals, rehabilitation centers, and health programs of other institutions. Since such data are often unavailable to lay persons, the doctor serves as coordinator of all medical information. Even though it may be impossible for the college physician to see each applicant personally prior to admission, he should interview every student for whom there is any evidence of a health problem. Such evidence may appear in answers to health questions on application forms, reports from high schools and other colleges, and the self-report of applicants and their parents. Wherever possible, the college physician should satisfy himself that there is no evidence of a major health problem in the case of any applicant accepted for admission. When it is determined that a major health problem is present, the physician should examine the student and discuss the matter with him before administrative decisions are made.

Some means of communication should be devised through which the physician communicates his findings to other participants in the admissions process. If the health problem is minor or not significant, the physician needs merely to send a card or form indicating this. On the other hand, if a health problem of importance is discovered, referral should be made to the counselor and a "hold" form should be sent to the admissions office. This "hold" notice would indicate that further admissions procedures should be held in abeyance until subsequent steps determine the status of the applicant. These subsequent steps may include interviews with the college counselors, conferences with the admissions personnel, and, possibly, consideration by the admissions committee.

The Counseling Office

The professional college counseling service plays a crucial role in the admissions procedure for physically handicapped students. The counselor prepares analyses of the total functioning of referred applicants with significant physical handicaps, as identified by the physician. His fundamental contribution is a determination of the way in which a disabled applicant manages his disability. It was previously noted that the objective medical determination of the type of handicap and its severity are merely starting points for understanding the actual limitations. Individuals with the same degree of loss of vision, hearing, mobility, manipulation, or vigor may function quite differently in learning situations. Less tangible factors of motivation, personality adjustment, and use of rehabilitation services often create differences in effectiveness among individuals with similar physical conditions.

In this frame of reference, the counselor attempts to analyze the variables which influence possible adaptability to the college environment. Whereas the physician notes the degree of mobility, the counselor reports on the actual use of legs and feet in typical life situations. The doctor may record objective findings relating to vision as reflected in vision tests and medical history. The counselor attempts to learn how the vision is used in daily life activities, the conditions under which vision is most and least effective, and the student's attitude toward his loss of vision. The counselor's search for data reaches beyond the doctor's office and the laboratory into the life space of the individual. The counselor is not qualified to arrive at diagnoses of physical conditions; he is competent to observe and report on function as demonstrated in everyday activities.

When an applicant is referred by the college physician, the counselor studies his application form, his high school record, and other data gathered by the admissions office. With the physician he reviews the medical information and ascertains the medically derived facts bearing on the admissions problem. Following this, the counselor interviews the student in an unstructured, warm, permissive atmosphere and endeavors to establish a relationship with him. An attempt is made to determine the self-concept of the student, the techniques he is using to solve life problems, and his attitude toward his disability. He is given an opportunity to discuss his life plans, the meaning of college attendance to him, and the way in which he handles the real limitations imposed by his disability.

Within the limits of one interview, the counselor attempts to assess the personality configuration of the applicant. If he suspects the existence of a serious emotional problem in addition to the physical handicap, he may consult the clinical psychologist, the psychiatrist, or other specialists designated by the institution. Usually, the counselor, by reason of his training and experience, can make a gross estimate of the emotional stability of the applicant.

After the student has discussed himself and his plans at some length, the counselor moves into a structured interview pattern which focuses on the functional abilities and limitations of the student. In a number of instances, this structure is provided by a set of forms, expressly devised for this purpose.

Stuart [54] suggests a schedule to be used in analyzing the physical demands of various college curricula. Earlier in this chapter (pages 61 to 65), sample forms were presented which assist in analyzing the student. When this aspect of the interview has been completed, the counselor inquires if the student has had previous counseling and/or rehabilitation service. If so, the sources of such help are noted and permission is requested to communicate with them. In almost all cases, the student and his parents are asked to sign release forms which authorize other agencies and individuals to share their data with the college. If the student and the parents grant permission, letters are sent to professional persons and institutions which have had contacts with the applicant. They are asked to assist the college in serving the student properly through giving the counselor access to needed information.

As a final step in this interview, the counselor attempts to strengthen his relationship with the student, answering any questions which the applicant may raise, and leaving the way open for subsequent counseling contacts. Although these functions do fall within the admissions function, per se, they are professional responsibilities of all counselors. Finally, the counselor informs the student of his status in the admissions procedure and the steps which remain to be taken before a final decision is made.

After all data have been gathered, the counselor prepares a summary report, briefly ordering the relevant facts and suggesting hypotheses about the student and his disability.

The Admissions Office and the Admissions Committee

Initially, the admissions office functions in the case of students with severe physical disabilities as it does with all students. The necessary application forms are distributed to applicants, transcripts are obtained, admissions interviews are conducted, admissions tests are given, and references from principals, teachers, and others in the student's home community are obtained. If possible, questions are included in the application blank which ask the applicant to report health problems. When high school and personal references are contacted, they are asked to report physical conditions which might affect the student's academic objectives. Finally, the student is asked to submit a medical examination report from his personal physician. These reports are then submitted to the college physician who screens them and selects cases for further study. Until his report is received, it is wise to delay admissions decisions.

The admissions office makes an initial decision on the basis of the data on academic eligibility. If the student is clearly ineligible, he is rejected without further study. If admission is doubtful on academic grounds, further study by the physician, counselor, and admissions board is suspended until the academic factors are clarified. If the student is clearly eligible for admission on academic grounds but has a suspected medical condition which warrants further study, he is referred to the college physician, and possibly, later, to the college counselor.

In essence, the admissions office collects relevant academic data and initial indications of health problems. Following the usual procedures, admissions officers ascertain academic eligibility. At that point, admission becomes dependent on data relating to the health problem, in accordance with the policies and procedures established by the institution.

In a number of colleges severely handicapped applicants and others are considered by an admissions committee. The most common types are a general admissions committee and a special admissions board for physically handicapped applicants.

GENERAL ADMISSIONS COMMITTEE. Most colleges and universities have an admissions committee or its equivalent which, among other functions, considers special admissions problems. These may concern students with doubtful credentials who apply for advanced standing, students with borderline secondary school records, and physically handicapped applicants. In the latter instance, the data gathered about each student is presented to the college-wide admissions committee which then considers the ramifications of the case. Such a committee may have the physician, the counselor, and the admissions officer as members, or it may use them as consultants. The advantage of this approach is that it treats physically handicapped students the same as other students with admissions problems. However, such a committee often lacks the time and specialized knowledge to make an exhaustive study of disabled students.

SPECIAL ADMISSIONS BOARD FOR PHYSICALLY HANDICAPPED APPLICANTS. Some institutions have constituted permanent committees for the sole purpose of considering the problems of handicapped applicants for admission. These committees are either subcommittees of the general admissions committee or autonomous groups reporting to the college administration. In either event, the membership will ordinarily include the physician, the counselor, admissions officers, members of the administration, and representatives of the faculty. This type of committee organization has the advantages of focusing its total effort on this special group and of having specialists in this area on its membership. The disadvantage is that it segregates the problems of disabled students from general admissions problems, thereby setting a precedent for similar action in other college activities.

Regardless of the type of committee organization used, the process employed is similar. The physician, the counselor, and/or the admissions officer identifies applicants whose severity of disability raises admissions problems of greater than customary difficulty. The cases of these applicants are referred to the committee. At the committee meeting, the physician, the counselor, and the admissions officer present the data which they have obtained bearing on the admissions problem. After discussion, a decision is arrived at which seems to represent the consensus of feeling within the group. This decision is an advisory one. It is the responsibility of the administration to make the final decision on admissions and to inform the applicant of that decision. Most often, the administration confirms the committee report and takes the necessary steps to implement it. A number of types of decision may be reached:

Unequivocal acceptance. In this instance, the student is accepted without conditions and becomes a regular student of the institution.

Probationary acceptance. An applicant may be accepted for a semester to ascertain through direct experience his level of functioning in the institution.

Conditional acceptance. The student is accepted on condition that he meet certain requirements in the period intervening between the date of acceptance and the date of enrollment. For physically handicapped students, the conditions may include obtaining further rehabilitation service, improving communications skills, developing greater facility in the activities of daily living, obtaining treatment for a remediable health condition, improving control over such disabilities as diabetes or epilepsy, and changing such aids as spectacles, artificial limbs, and crutches. At the time of enrollment, the student is re-examined and, if he has met the conditions, is accepted unconditionally.

Delayed consideration. When a health condition requires lengthy or extensive remediation, the student may be informed that his application will be considered again after the process has been completed. Thus, the prospect of serious surgery would lead to a postponement of committee consideration. This would also hold true of a possible lengthy period of convalescence, or of rehabilitation, such as extensive re-training needed in learning to write left-handed after disablement of the right arm, or the development of new communications skills in learning esophageal speech after surgical removal of the larynx. In any event, the student may re-apply later when his situation will be re-examined in the light of his new status.

Rejection. If the committee decides, on the basis of a detailed examination, that the institution cannot serve the applicant adequately, the administration informs him of the reasons for the action.

In all circumstances, provision should be made for a counseling interview subsequent to the transmittal of the administrative decision on admission to the applicant. In this interview, the applicant will have opportunity to express his feelings about the decision and to make plans for his future. If he has been accepted, he can discuss the conditions and limitations placed on him with the counselor. For example, some institutions require that disabled students undergo periodic medical examinations and/or subsequent re-evaluations by the special committee which handles physically handicapped students.[1] If the student's application has been rejected or deferred, he may wish to learn the mechanics of filing an appeal. Many institutions have formalized machinery for such appeals and the counselor is often delegated to assist the student in preparing his request for a reconsideration of his application.

A counseling interview subsequent to the administrative decision on admission has the value of reinforcing the counseling relationship so that it may be most effectively used by the accepted

---

[1] These committees may be called health guidance boards, medical advisory committees, or handicapped students guidance committees.

applicant in his later college experience. It also lays the groundwork for a mutual understanding of the type of academic and other supervision which may be planned for him. In this way, the student learns what is expected of him and how he may discharge his responsibilities.

Where the number of severely disabled students applying for admission to an institution is small, it may seem that the considerations and procedures suggested are unduly elaborate. In some instances, the steps may be telescoped or modified to meet the needs of the institution. However, this much is clear: Increasing numbers of disabled students will be applying for admission at most colleges. The best way to meet the problem and to offer maximum educational service is by having a rational policy based on well-conceived admissions procedures.

Curricular and Extra- | 4
curricular Activities for
Physically Handicapped
College Students

A VAST AMOUNT of analysis, committee work, and administrative decision making enters into the formulation of the typical college curriculum. It is an expression of the concept of the college mission, put together as a product of the massed effort of various components of an institution. Through it, the goals and philosophy of the college are implemented and given shape. Since it is so vital an expression of the nature of the college program, it is not readily susceptible to major change on behalf of individual students. An overhauling of a college plan of study is a highly serious matter, undertaken only after clear evidence of need and exhaustive consideration. Since changes in curriculum are not made lightly, the institution is likely to be cautious in admitting students who may require important modifications in the program. Obviously, these individual modifications cannot be accorded the intensive consideration that is given to changes in the total program. To do anything less—to make changes without intensive study—is often resisted by college personnel.

APPROACHES TO CURRICULUM PROBLEMS

Confronted by the academic and social needs of severely disabled students, colleges and universities have generally followed one or more of three patterns in handling the problem: exclusion, laissez faire, and modification.

EXCLUSION. If it is believed that the disabled student is unable to function adequately in the subject matter of a learning experience, or that he is incapable of performing certain tasks, or

79

that he constitutes a safety hazard in certain respects, the experience will be omitted from his program. As a rule, if he is excluded from one or more aspects of a total field, the remaining aspects, which may be well within his physical capacities, will also be omitted from his program, especially in subjects in which one course builds on another. Usually, plans for supplementation or substitution are not made.

LAISSEZ FAIRE. When the disabled student is admitted to the activity, no effort is made to adapt it to his needs. He is left to sink or swim. If he develops his own resources for coping with the situation, he may salvage a great deal from it. On the other hand, if he cannot adjust to the given reality, he fails. Institutions which adopt this laissez-faire technique are inclined to hold disabled students more or less firmly to the existing curriculum, with few attempts to waive certain learning experiences.

MODIFICATION. If it is determined that a student, because of physical problems, cannot function adequately in a particular area, one of two steps may be taken. The student may be admitted to the activity after certain modifications in its structure have made it possible for him to compete successfully and to acquire the desired learning. Or the institution may waive a particular requirement and, after careful consideration, prescribe another which is considered an adequate substitute. In effect, the institution takes responsibility for reducing barriers to the student that are inherent in its regular curriculum. Ideally, these modifications do not result in a lowering of standards. They are essentially ways of circumventing a barrier, achieving mastery of a subject-matter area through slightly different means.

To clarify these three patterns the examples presented below are drawn from three areas of the curriculum which often present problems to disabled students and to those who work with them on the college level.

Physical Education

EXCLUSION. The disabled student is not permitted to take any physical education. He is not given any credit for it nor is he penalized because it has been waived.

LAISSEZ FAIRE. The disabled student is enrolled in regular physical education courses. No special plan is set up for him. He may be used for routine tasks in the physical education office or other casual activities not related to physical education needs. If he performs the irrelevant activities which are assigned to him, he will probably receive a passing grade for the course.

MODIFICATION. The disabled student has needs for physical education that are as compelling as those of the nondisabled student. In some cases, retention of gains achieved through rehabilitation may depend on continual conditioning. The activities which are most suitable for him in physical education can be readily ascertained through consultation with the physician and the rehabilitation center. Instead of requiring him to perform the activities established in the regular physical education curriculum, the college provides a program of individualized and controlled exercise consistent with the medical recommendations. Thus, the student not only achieves the benefits of physical education but he realizes that, like other students, he is expected to participate in the mental and physical activities that the college offers.

Laboratory Sciences

EXCLUSION. The disabled student is not assigned to laboratory sections in the sciences in which he enrolls. He may be permitted to attend lecture and recitation sections but must rely on the laboratory notes of other students. The exclusion may be so complete that he is not permitted to observe other students in the laboratory. The basis for this total exclusion from the laboratory may be a fear that his very presence constitutes a hazard. This exclusion is based on the possibility of emergency situations involving scalding liquids or caustic solutions in which the student would have to move quickly in order to escape injury. Since some severely disabled students cannot do this, exclusion is perceived as the alternative.

LAISSEZ FAIRE. Regardless of the student's limitations, he is permitted to enter any laboratory section for which he is academically qualified. No attempt is made to assess his capacities for performing the required activities. As in the case of any student, he is expected to perform and record his laboratory work. If he cannot do so, he makes his own arrangements for help from other students or fails the course. Through observing the work of another student he sets up an informal partnership and attempts to keep step with the rest of the class in laboratory requirements, some of which are beyond his physical capacities.

MODIFICATION.   The instructor and student assess the physical requirements of the laboratory experiments. Those which are within the student's capacities are retained intact in the program, and those which go beyond his physical resources are modified. Among the modifications employed may be teamwork with other students and the substitution of certain experiments, techniques, equipment, and materials. If absolutely necessary, the disabled student will be excused from certain activities which are obviously impossible or hazardous.

Speech

EXCLUSION.   The speech handicapped student is excluded from speech courses, conversational foreign language experiences, and all other activities which require normal speech. It is believed that speech work exposes such individuals to tension, frustration, and tasks which are beyond their limits.

LAISSEZ FAIRE.   The speech handicapped student is enrolled in all required speech courses. However, little if any regard is paid to his special needs or to his capabilities for meeting the demands of the course. As a result, instructors tend to interpret the situation for themselves. Some find the student obviously unable to meet class standards and fail him or urge him to withdraw. Others set up a frame of reference based largely on sympathy and grade the student on effort.

MODIFICATION.   Many disabled students have strong needs for speech education which reach far beyond exposure to the typical speech or language course. These needs can be met either by providing specialized individual speech work or modifying the required speech courses. In the latter case, the student's communications problems are analyzed. In consultation with a speech therapist, if possible, classroom activities are set up which will benefit the student without subjecting him to ridicule or to excessively frustrating situations.

Exclusion, laissez faire, and modification may exist side by side in the same institution. This often occurs in the absence of a firm institutional policy, and when it does, each department head and administrative officer adopts the attitude which seems most appropriate for him and his departmental situation. If applied on a rational basis, all three patterns have their place in a college and may contribute to the over-all program for severely disabled students. In effect, it is impossible to state that one of the three is superior to the others. Each has its place and, if used differentially, adds depth to the academic program.

Exclusion is exceedingly helpful when it is objectively established that participation in an activity will be physically impossible for the student, harmful to him, or hazardous to others around him. There are times when the severely disabled student must be excluded. For example, an art appreciation course based on museum observations lies outside the experiential capacities of the blind student just as music appreciation work is clearly beyond the hearing capacities of the deaf student. Furthermore, any type of physical education is contraindicated for the student with a health problem of such a nature that the physician has restricted his classroom activities to a minimum. A serious cardiac problem is a case in point. In addition, an epileptic student who has relatively frequent grand mal seizures despite good medical care and medication should not be entrusted with cooperative laboratory work in chemistry where his possible loss of consciousness may result in harm to others.

Though exclusion has a place in arranging a curriculum for a physically handicapped college student, great caution must be exercised in barring the door to any activity. If, despite every attempt at adjustment, it becomes clear that nothing further can be done to safeguard the disabled student and/or his classmates, the alternative is exclusion. But exclusion should be a last resort. Every effort should be made to be certain that the decision is based on rational considerations rather than on the feelings of the individuals concerned.

Laissez faire has a place, too. When it is clear that the well-being of a student is not involved, laissez faire may be selectively used to assist a disabled person to attain a more realistic self-concept. Some physically disabled students have distorted concepts of their abilities. Their levels of aspiration and their goals may be grossly understated or overstated. The professional educator may know this and attempt to plan an educational program more consistent with the student's actual capacities only to meet with strong student resistance. Since the student does not see himself as the educator does, he may not understand the reason for certain exclusions or modifications in program. In following through a four-year educational program with a severely disabled student, it is essential that the college and the student share similar perceptions of the physical capacities of the latter. If not, there may be misunderstanding and friction throughout the student's college career. Thus, the educator may be reasonably certain that the course of action he is planning for the student is the most advisable one, but he may find it necessary to accept a less desirable program in order to promote student growth.

If a student's self-concept is at variance with the best thinking of the professional personnel working with him it is a serious deterrent to education. Generally, two major methods are used to attempt to modify an "unreal" self-concept. The first is counseling which will be discussed in a subsequent chapter. The other method is environmental manipulation. In our frame of reference, this may be achieved by permitting the student to structure his program in terms of what he conceives his capacities to be. Obviously, this can only be done if the student's decisions are congruent with college policy and are medically approved.

Let us assume that a blind student wishes to take college algebra without tutoring assistance, or a student with cerebral palsy and exceedingly limited mobility elects a course in geology which demands frequent strenuous field trips. In discussing these choices with the student, the counselor or the administrator may discover that the student earnestly believes that he can function in the situation. Furthermore, it appears that this student belief is part of a delusional system he has built around his disability. In an effort to help the student to assess the validity of his self-concept, the college may assume a laissez-faire attitude. It may permit the student to enter the experience on his own terms, following him up to rescue him from difficulty, if necessary. This method is helpful if the college makes professional counseling help available to the student to enable him to evaluate each experience and to make the changes in his self-concept which seem warranted by the consequences of his behavior. In many cases, a single experience may not have the desired result. A series of events may be needed, each supplemented by an opportunity for the student to discuss the experience.

Laissez faire is also useful in another way. A number of disabled students, after initial help, are quite capable of self-direction in the college environment. They have a sense of reality about their disabilities and the limits within which they function. Their decisions are mature ones, consistent with college policy and their own capacities, and the intervention of college personnel may be minimal. It is often advisable to reduce service to such students almost to the vanishing point. Unless a crisis occurs and they are referred for service by faculty members or seek help on their own initiative, their best interests are served by letting them work out their own problems. Thus, a realistic laissez-faire program, limited to disabled students who can function successfully in such a climate, promotes independence and self-reliance. It is hoped that students who are currently not able to operate in this way can be assisted through the college services to approach this ideal.

Modification often has face validity and is awarded social approbation. There is something praiseworthy about the idea of a college or university modifying its program to meet the needs of a severely disabled student. In most cases, this is really so. Yet it should be noted that there are occasions when modification can be destructive. One of these is when college standards are compromised and less is demanded of an individual because he is physically handicapped. These lesser requirements, sometimes concealed under the guise of modification, are not really necessary within the true limits of the disability. They may be made to please a parent, a student, or a faculty member, to avoid community pressure, or to sidestep facing the basic issue of the type of service which the institution should be offering to severely disabled students.

In some cases, modifications in curriculum are made at the student's urging. Some disabled students have had a lifetime of training in dependency, and in the college, as in other situations, they reach out for favors and relaxation of rules. Not infrequently, the disability is used as a wedge for acquiring special privileges. If an institution succumbs to this type of seduction and pressure, it may be merely avoiding a difficult situation. The ultimate best interests of the disabled student often depend on his being required to perform realistically within his limits. Attempts to cajole, excite pity, and exert pressure should be resisted. If a college or university has made a careful medical, social, and psychological study of the disabled student, it may safely set up requirements for him as it does for all other students. In doing this, it can assist some disabled students to discard the disability as a way of influencing authority and reducing competition. Thus, modifications should be made only when a good authenticated case can be made for them. Otherwise, they may become a vehicle for the expression of neurotic needs by some physically handicapped students.

In essence, then, exclusion, laissez faire, and modification are components of a battery of tools used by the college and university in curriculum building for the disabled student. In no case should any of the three be used to water down existing standards. However, in the framework of college policies and procedures, all may be used at different times to implement the philosophy of the institution, to provide the disabled student with a sound curriculum, and to promote his maturity. Skillful, selective use of these three methods demands teamwork within the college and a counseling service which can assist the student in developing insight and a realistic self-concept.

SPECIAL CURRICULUM PROBLEMS

Examinations, Norms, and Grades

Disabled students should be required to take examinations planned for all other students. Occasionally, severely impaired students have been exempted from examinations, or given substitute assignments such as preparing special papers. There is little justification for this course of action. The adjustments should not be made in the nature of the test, but in the manner of administering it. With the help of an amanuensis and flexible time limits, virtually any disabled student is capable of managing the physical aspects of a test. If he is not able to do so, real questions may be raised about his capacity for college-level work. Generally speaking, instructors need not make such major adjustments as preparing special equivalent forms, having Braille transcribed into inkprint, or administering the test himself. In most cases, the student assumes the responsibility for making the necessary arrangements and for obtaining an approved person to serve as an amanuensis. Ideally, the disabled student takes the test at the same time as the other students and submits his finished paper at the end of the examination period.

This general procedure cannot be followed under all circumstances. For example, it is not adapted to "surprise" quizzes, frequent short classroom tests, and group oral examinations. When these techniques are used, substitute measures may have to be found for some severely disabled students. Furthermore, when a test is prepared with a speed factor in mind, it should be remembered that many disabled students are likely to be slower in completing it because of their physical limitations and the techniques used in administering it. Thus, when a 50-item objective test is read to a blind student, the oral reading will require more time than the silent reading by other students. Or if a student with severe hand limitations dictates his essay test responses to an amanuensis, this may require more time than if he himself typed or wrote the answers.

In the administration of standardized intelligence, personality, and aptitude tests, some use is made of special norms set up for the disability group representing the student. Thus, in scoring the Minnesota Rate of Manipulation Test, special norms are used in comparing the performance of a blind student with other blind persons who have taken the test. Similar approaches are common with other disability groups. It should be clearly noted at this time that the procedure of using sets of special norms is not universal nor unanimously accepted among rehabilitation psychologists and counselors. However, in a college or university, there is little room for special norms for disabled students.

The academic performance of a disabled student must be evaluated in the commonly accepted framework of the institution. If absolute standards are maintained by the instructor, the products of the disabled student's work must be measured against that yardstick. If relative standards are used (i.e., marking on a curve), the disabled student must take his place in that relative set of values. Perhaps the greatest disservice to the physically handicapped student is to inflate his grade by applying a unique standard to his work or to penalize him in an unwarranted way for work that is adequately performed under modified conditions. By the time he reaches college age, the disabled student should be prepared to work within the matrix established by our society for nondisabled persons. During his early school years, the atypical disabled student may find himself assessed in terms based on his individual capacities and potentialities. However, this can only be a phase of his educational experience. Sooner or later, he must come to grips with the standards that govern other people. By the time he reaches college, he should have had considerable experience in conforming to external standards. If not, he may have to make a rapid adaptation to such standards or find himself unprepared to go on, even if an institution mistakenly is willing to accept less from him than from other students.

In the same way, colleges should maintain a realistic attitude toward grades. In some cases, disabled students are marked on the basis of real achievement tempered by sympathy, tolerance, or pity. These emotions have no place in grading. A disservice is done to the disabled student when he is allowed to believe that his work is better than it really is. Such misplaced "kindness" may deprive the student of an opportunity to really evaluate his academic capacities. Occasionally, it is not so much emotion which distorts a disabled student's grade as it is a desire on the part of the instructor to play the role of therapist. He may actually believe that a successful experience in the classroom will influence the student's personality development. The effects of such an action are complex and, for the lay person, relatively unpredictable. The college classroom is not designed for psychotherapy but for learning. Grades should represent actual performance rather than be used as a tool to evoke desired forms of student behavior.

In summary, it is clear that modifications in examinations should never be in content, but only in administration. Whatever adjustments are made, they should never be in norms or grades. Disabled students, in some cases, may be expected to do things differently. However, the nature of the learning and the goals to be achieved should parallel that of other students. No compromise is possible in this area.

Readings, Research, and Papers

The principle governing student achievement has already been laid down. Even blind students, who may have problems in coping with the volume of reading required on the college level, should be expected to complete *all* reading assignments. It is assumed that every reading assignment given by the instructor is essential to the student's learning, and there is no room for compromise on this point. It is a fact that many blind students, as well as those with perceptual or language limitations, find it difficult to complete these assignments. However, the successful disabled student devotes more time to his reading, takes a curtailed academic program, and/or develops techniques for skimming that enable him to function adequately. Even in situations where heavier than average reading requirements are maintained, as in history, literature, and law courses, blind students are able to keep pace. The process of doing so involves considerable sacrifice and a willingness to postpone immediate satisfaction, but it can be done.

Much the same can be said about research and papers required in some college courses. Preparation of papers and participation of students in research are considered important learning experiences. Excluding disabled students for any reason, however well intentioned, denies them the opportunity to learn. In some instances, particularly in laboratory research projects, modifications may be necessary. However, in accordance with principles stated earlier, these should be made only when absolutely necessary and should be of a nature designed to retain the essential character of the learning experience.

Choice of a Major Field

Many institutions require the student to select a major field, usually in the sophomore or junior year. This is a key decision in the student's collegiate career since it marks his area of specialization and, to some extent, helps to draw career lines and suggest the focus of graduate work. Students become conscious of the significance of this decision and invest a great deal of thought, often seeking guidance to assist them in their choices. Some institutions simply accept the student's choice of major as long as he meets the academic requirements established for it in terms of prerequisites and quality of work. Other institutions require that the student be accepted by the department in question, which considers all applicants, basing their decision on criteria deemed relevant to successful work in the area. Both approaches create problems in the education of the severely disabled college student.

If the institution accepts the student's choice of major, and if he meets minimum educational qualifications, it may be confronted by students whose needs will demand extensive modification in the requirements. As extreme cases in point, a speech handicapped student may select a major in speech, or a student with a manual limitation may select laboratory sciences which require extensive manipulation of laboratory equipment, or a multiply involved cerebral palsy student may select teaching—a field in which it is improbable that he will find employment. In the above instances, it may seem reasonable to permit the student in question to major in the area he chooses. However, to do so automatically, without extensive discussion and analysis, is unwise.

Consideration should be given to the physical demands of work in a major field. Basically, the question to be answered is: "Can a program of study be established in this field for a disabled student with the specific limitations noted and will this program provide the essential learning experiences without extensive deletions and dilutions in the curriculum?" If, after careful study, the answer is in the affirmative, the college may move ahead in drawing up a program for the student. On the other hand, if serious reservations are expressed, it may be necessary to work out the situation with the student, using community rehabilitation consultants if necessary. There are some instances in which pursuit of a particular major can be established as undesirable. If this conclusion is based on rational grounds, supported by consultative opinion, then the student should not be permitted to major in this area. Obviously, some students will resist this decision. When this occurs, they should be offered two resources: the right of appeal through stated administrative channels, and an opportunity to discuss the matter with a professional counselor.

If students are screened by the various college departments, each using its own criteria, similar problems may be encountered. Some departments, moved by sympathy, may be too uncritical of the capacities of the disabled students; others may exclude them too readily. In either case, students, faculty, and administration may become enmeshed in problems of implementing the institutional policies for severely disabled students.

Departmental heads and committees often vary in their feelings about physically handicapped students. Some may reveal maudlin sentimentality; others, realistic acceptance; still others, overt or covert rejection. These attitudes are reflections of those held by people in general but, unlike people in general, departmental heads and committees have important decision-making functions relative to students. If these attitudes becloud rational decisions, they create problems for the student and the college administration. Some administrations will support departmental decisions almost without exception. In such cases, departmental personnel with negative feelings about disabled students, or unrealistic perceptions of their abilities, may grant or deny admission to some students where such action is not warranted by the facts. When this occurs, the major recourse is long-range refashioning of attitudes, whenever possible.

The author recalls a department head who adamantly refused admission as a major in his department to a severely disabled, cerebral palsied youth although there was evidence that the student could function successfully in the department. Perhaps the most persuasive of such evidence was the fact that the student had taken a few courses in the department by special permission of one of the instructors. The teacher considered this student to be one of the most promising he had ever encountered, and conveyed this information to the department chairman, suggesting that the young man be admitted as a major. There was a considerable amount of discussion in the department about the case. When some of the student's papers were published in professional journals, he was given access to additional departmental offerings by individual instructors. His performance was so convincing that he was permitted to enroll as a minor in the department. However, he was not permitted to major in the field.

Attitudes are deeply rooted in the personality of the individual, and are relatively resistant to change. In the college community one is likely to find faculty members whose negative attitudes toward severely disabled students are persistent. Sometimes they recognize the existence of these attitudes, and function overtly in ways consistent with their beliefs. At other times they disclaim such attitudes but behave in ways which suggest their existence. Working with such faculty members is often a difficult experience for disabled students. It is recognized that occasionally these students misinterpret instructor behavior and perceive bias where it really does not exist. On the other hand, they are quite sensitive to rejection, and recognize it in its various guises.

Sometimes disabled students approach counselors or administrative officers of the college, demanding immediate redress of what they believe to be prejudice against them. In almost every instance these prove to be difficult cases to handle. At the very least the information should be shared with the faculty member in question, if the student agrees to this. In most cases the faculty member deals with the problem in a rational fashion, working the situation through with the student in a helpful and friendly manner. If the faculty member responds emotionally, resolution of the problem becomes increasingly difficult.

If the problem really lies in the attitudinal framework of the faculty member, his attitudes are not likely to change rapidly. Administrators have found that the most effective technique is to expose the staff member gradually to contacts with disabled students in a satisfying context. The chairman of a mathematics department, for example, responded negatively to visually handicapped students and was unable to see how they could function in her area. When a partially seeing student, gifted in mathematics, attracted the attention of faculty members in the department, the chairman became acquainted with her and was equally impressed with her ability. When the time arrived for deciding on a major, the counselor reviewed the medical evidence with the student to ascertain if mathematics constituted a realistic field in view of its possible impact on her vision. When the department head heard of this, she made inquiries of the counselor, hoping that the medical data would not contraindicate mathematics as a major field. The contact with this student was satisfying for the chairman and led to her acceptance of other partially seeing students. She has not yet moved to an acceptance of totally blind students, but the chances of her doing so are better now.

Logical arguments are not altogether successful in modifying overly accepting or unrealistically rejecting attitudes. As indicated previously, forceful dynamic leadership in the college often sets the tone. If the top administrative officers take a stand and interpret the mission of the institution to serve intellectually capable students, disabled or not, changes in attitude will come about more easily. If, on the other hand, the administration is content to allow department chairmen and committees to decide whom they should educate, some inequities may be anticipated. If decisions of this kind are to be left in departmental hands, it would seem wise to set up some type of appeal machinery. Once a student has been accepted by a college or university, the institution has a responsibility to make available to him all the learning resources that are at the disposal of other students providing he is capable of meeting the requirements and will not be a safety hazard to other students. Exclusion must be based on considerations other than the feelings of individual staff members.

Special Programming

The programming needs of some severely disabled students may require curriculum adjustments. Daily schedules should be prepared only after consideration of the health requirements of the individual. Students with arrested tuberculosis may have a study tolerance of less than a full day. As a result, their work load must be restricted to a lower than average number of classroom hours. Also, it may be recommended that their courses be concentrated in the morning or afternoon to permit prescribed rest periods. For cardiac students who require frequent rest periods throughout the day, courses should be spaced at least one hour apart to provide the necessary periods of limited activity.

Students with transportation problems may require a variety of program adjustments. The use of the family car, limousine service, or special transportation may involve different times of arrival and departure. If possible, courses should be scheduled to agree with these hours. Another scheduling problem centers around the location of classes. Schedules should be devised to minimize travel from one building to another or to limit classes to buildings which are easily accessible. If a disabled student is re-

ceiving medical care or treatment through one of the medically al-
lied therapies his programming should take into account the times
of these appointments. For some disabled students, these treatments may be essential to maintain current health status.

The actual mechanics of programming may be performed in a
variety of ways. A common approach is for the physician and the
college counselor to specify the needs of the student and to suggest
the type of schedule adjustments which seem most advisable.
These recommendations are sent to the registrar's office which
studies the practicality of fulfilling them.

Early registration of severely disabled students is another de-
vice that is found helpful. Under this plan, a selected group
of students registers at some time prior to the regular registration
period. Usually, this small group of handicapped students will be
served by one or more counselors, registration personnel, and student assistants. When registration is organized in this way, without the pressure of large numbers of other students, officers find it
possible to provide highly individualized assistance. Also, since
all classes are "open," it is possible to select the sections best
adapted to individual needs. Another advantage of early registration is that it reduces the possibility of overexertion on the part of
students with health problems. Typically, registration demands a
certain amount of waiting in line, moving from place to place, and
obtaining a number of permissions and authorizations. Early registration can be planned so that the physical demands of the registration process are adjusted to the capacities of the registrants.
Thus, students with cardiac problems, asthma, and other health
conditions are spared the strenuous demands of some registration
procedures. Experience indicates that a large majority of disabled
students do not need early registration. However, for the few who
do, it is an important service.

Professional Programs

Many undergraduate schools offer professional preparation in
a number of fields. The most common of these is teaching. Others
include nursing, engineering, business, law, agriculture, journalism,
dramatics, and so on. Each of these professional curricula has
its own matrix of requirements. Each is faced with the problem

of admitting severely physically handicapped students. Some of the problems that arise will be discussed with particular reference to teaching. Education has been selected because it enrolls more students in undergraduate work than other professional fields and because it illustrates these problems with special coherence. The remarks made about teaching will be relevant to other undergraduate and graduate professional areas of preparation.

Teacher education programs have twin objectives: to prepare the most competent teachers possible, and to help students meet state and local certification and licensing provisions. The two objectives are usually congruent, but occasionally the staff of a teacher education program has concepts of how teachers should be educated that are at variance with governmental requirements. In most cases, the institution attempts to implement its own best thinking about the matter, while meeting the demands of licensure and certification. Despite the most earnest desires of education departments, the education curriculum cannot ignore these requirements. If it does, its graduates may be denied opportunities to teach, and the community may be deprived of the services of promising young teachers.

Most states do not stipulate the minimum physical requirements for teaching, but some municipalities do. In New York City, for example, attempts have been made to stipulate the physical capacities required in teaching and to exclude candidates who fail to meet these standards. As in every code of this type, much of the content is reasonable and consistent with sound analyses of physical demands. There is always a tendency to enforce such a code to the strict letter of the law. As a result, some quite capable applicants are rejected for reasons which are irrelevant to their teaching performance.

Even when a school system fails to state its physical requirements, these are implicit in its hiring practices. The local superintendent of schools and other hiring officials are likely to have their own concepts of the physical limitations which they will accept in candidates for positions. Not infrequently, these requirements are vague and half-formed. Sometimes, they have little logical basis. For example, a candidate who has had tuberculosis, but is now medically approved for full-day activity, may still find prejudice expressed against him in a number of school systems. Realistic or not, teaching applicants will find that many disabilities are real barriers to employment.

In considering applicants for admission to a teacher education program, college staffs are often faced with the dilemma of the candidate who gives evidence of teaching potentialities but who will have very great difficulty in finding employment. A typical example is that of a student with a marked speech handicap. Some school systems will reject such a candidate on the grounds that his speech defect may be imitated by the children and appear in their speech patterns. Furthermore, it is feared that he will have difficulty in communicating to the children in his classes. In view of these problems, should a teacher education program admit such a student?

The complexity of the issue is compounded by the fact that there are severely disabled teachers functioning at all educational levels. For example, a survey has revealed that there are some fifty blind persons teaching in high schools in the United States. Some school systems have on their teaching staffs individuals who would not be acceptable as new employees today. In some cases, the disabilities were contracted during the teaching career in the system. Even a system like New York City's Board of Education employs numerous teachers with health problems. Apparently, despite these health problems, they are able to carry out their teaching duties. Yet, if they were now to appear for physical examination preparatory to entering the system, they would be excluded.

A further complicating factor is that some disabled students do not fully accept statements made by education departments regarding the probable difficulties they will have in finding teaching jobs. The tendency is for them to focus on those few unusual persons who have succeeded despite severe disabilities. They perceive themselves as the exceptions rather than the general rule. After the course of training has been completed, a number of these students find that it has been in vain. Unable to find employment in their chosen field, they become bitter, frustrated, and hostile to the college which prepared them. Oftentimes, they complain that they were never fully informed about the possibilities, or they feel that despite their own insistence, the college should not have permitted them to go ahead.

The position of the education department is often a difficult one. However, it seems evident that their responsibilities are both in selecting and in guiding students. The department is responsible for selecting students who have the qualifications deemed necessary for the teaching function. These qualifications should be set only after careful study. They should reflect objective thinking about the physical, intellectual, and emotional demands of teaching. In part, they should be consistent with the policies of employers in the field, but not wholly slavish to them. Education departments have a responsibility for elevating the status of teaching and for developing increasingly rational standards of selection. A wholehearted and uncritical adherence to the prejudices of some employers may not be the optimum way of achieving this objective. Yet the realities of the employment situation cannot be altogether denied. Each department must somehow chart its own course. In doing so, it cannot ignore the fact that it is attempting to prepare teachers who will be sensitive to individual differences. Its own insensitivity to the individual differences of its students and applicants may belie some of the concepts taught in its classes. In fact, some colleges and universities prepare students to become special educators. They may prepare teachers of the visually handicapped, hearing handicapped, orthopedically disabled, and neurologically impaired. Yet such institutions may too readily refuse to accept persons with these disabilities for their own teacher education programs.

If the selection procedure is rational, the teacher education program can apply its physical standards to applicants without excessive sympathy or rejection. However, after rejecting a student, the teacher education program has the responsibility of discussing the basis for his rejection with him. Unless such counseling is provided, the student may continue to seek similar training elsewhere for a career in a field which specialists believe is not feasible for him. Some students will persist in their original plans despite such information and subsequent counseling. Others will gradually reorganize their goals and emerge from the experience with a more realistic self-concept. Teacher education programs thus have the dual responsibility of selection and guidance. Exclusion of positive and negative prejudice from both is necessary in assisting the disabled student prepare for his career.

EXTRACURRICULAR ACTIVITIES

A few colleges and universities have perceived the social needs of disabled students as being incapable of full satisfaction within the normal extracurricular social structure of the institution. Thus, they have established activities that are more or less segregated. In one case, it is a wheel-chair basketball team for paraplegics. In another, it is a club for handicapped students. In a third, it is the practice to have disabled students room together. Such arrangements are thought to have the advantage of structuring social situations in ways peculiarly suited to what are believed to be unique social needs. The disabled student has fewer opportunities to feel lonely, left out, and unwanted. Yet this procedure throws a mantle of protectiveness over him, denying him opportunities to learn social skills for himself and fashion his own social life on lines which appeal to him.

It is argued that one or more segregated activities supplement all the existing social activities in the college community. Instead of serving as replacements, they are said to broaden the program, for the disabled student may simultaneously engage in both integrated and segregated activities. There is, however, a kind of Gresham's law which operates in these situations. Experience in segregated recreational programs for deaf, blind, and orthopedically handicapped persons suggests that the provision of such facilities may increase isolation from social contacts with nonhandicapped persons. In other words, participation in these special recreational activities tends to cut down on participation in general recreational activities.

It is advisable to examine some of the reasons given for setting up special activities for handicapped students. Some say that it is necessary because disabled students cannot take part in activities open to other students. To a degree this is so. However, after eliminating the activities which are made impossible by the limits of the disability, many others remain. A blind student may not be able to participate in baseball or football, but he can function well in swimming and wrestling. In fact, a number of varsity wrestlers have been blind students. A deaf student may not be able to join the college band but he can dance, using vibrations as a guide, and he can participate in many sports. Gallaudet College, for example, fields a football team each fall. Orthopedically handicapped students may not be able to compete in varsity sports, but they can successfully take part in debating teams, dramatics, departmental clubs, and numerous other activities.

Many nonphysically handicapped students face limitations in their choice of activities. Relatively few individuals can succeed in all areas in which they choose to participate. Admittedly, the problem of the disabled student may be more intense, but it does not differ substantially in kind. Most students tend to find one or more extracurricular areas in which they can express themselves creatively. Sometimes they need help in doing so. When this happens, counselors in the office of the dean of students can be helpful. The problem for the physically limited student is not so much creating new activities built around his handicap as it is helping him find areas in the existing social structure in which he can feel accepted and successful. Obviously, this may be a challenging task in some cases.

Most of the disabled students enrolled in colleges and universities will live out their lives in the company of nonhandicapped persons. Among other disadvantages of segregated activities is the one which ignores the fact that the ultimate social success of the disabled adult must come in nonhandicapped society. The college campus should be a place in which training for this experience is given. This training is best offered through assisting the student to function adequately with his peers. The special club for the handicapped, the wheel-chair basketball team, and other segregated activities are temporary expedients at best. The day will come when the disabled person finds himself back in his home community where there is no concentration of disabled persons with like interests. The time to develop integrated interests is at college, where the training and counseling which may be needed in the process are readily available.

In a typical multifaceted college activity program there are probably a number of groups, clubs, and social units which are within the capacities of most physically disabled students and which will appeal to their interests. The barrier to participation is generally not the dearth of activities, but rather the psychological attitudes of the disabled student and his classmates. An important function of the institution's student personnel program is to assist the disabled student to understand the dynamics within him which may be preventing his integration into college life. Another function, equally important, is to help nondisabled students to a more wholesome acceptance of the disabled student.

Some physically limited students have been sheltered from extensive contacts with nondisabled peers. They may have been educated in isolation from them, or they may have been shielded by parents and teachers from the "give and take" of normal social relations. In either event, the student can benefit from social counseling which will help him become aware of the difficulties he is facing in social activities and of the satisfaction he may attain through controlled participation in a few carefully chosen activities. In some cases, the student's personality problems may present barriers so acute that the student will require psychotherapy or participation in rehabilitation group work activities.

On the other hand, the disabled student may have achieved a psychological readiness for entering a number of activities but has faced a certain amount of rejection on the part of other students. Once it has been ascertained that this rejection is real and generalized, the personnel worker may call on student leaders to help create a more favorable social situation for the disabled student. These instances are relatively rare. In most cases, young people find it easy to share experiences with physically handicapped students. If there is any danger in the situation it is in the direction of overprotectiveness and exploitation, although occasionally, a nondisabled student will express his own neurotic needs through symbiotic relationships with disabled classmates. Student personnel workers should be alert to this possibility and be ready to assist the students, through counseling, to develop healthier interpersonal relationships.

In this respect, it should be stressed that disabled students, like all other students, have certain rights to privacy. The presence of a disability does not give college staff personnel any special responsibility for the private social activities of such students. Help offered in the social area must follow the general principles of offering help in other areas. The student must retain the right to accept or reject this help without penalty. Sometimes, personnel workers become overly concerned with the personal problems of a disabled student, and may invade private areas of his life which he is entitled to keep inviolate. As long as he functions within the general framework of the institution and meets its requirements, the physically handicapped student should be free to ask for help when he needs it and to accept offers of help only when he feels this need.

Counseling Programs for the Physically Handicapped College Student

5

THE NEED FOR COUNSELING SERVICES in colleges and universities is now almost universally accepted. Gradually, the professionally trained counselor is supplementing the staff member who undertakes counseling as part of his instructional duties. In its simplest terms, counseling assists the student to meet a current problem and, in the process, hopes to prepare him to meet future problems more successfully with his own resources. The starting point in most college counseling services is the college environment. Either the student realizes, or those about him observe, that he is not making full use of his capacities, is not achieving satisfaction in his work and leisure, and is encountering difficulties in interpersonal relationships.

The college environment makes certain well-defined demands on the individual student. Most students succeed in adapting to this environment without specialized assistance. Through their own resources, or with some help from the faculty and the administration, they meet most of the challenges of college living. There are some students, however, who cannot "fit in" even though they exert every effort to do so. They find themselves underachieving, unhappy, and unfulfilled. Unless something specific is done to assist them, they will either require gross modifications in the college environment or withdraw from the institution. Counseling is not only a means of salvaging human resources; it is also a technique through which students become more effective and happier people.

Numerous textbooks on college counseling are available. This book will not attempt to duplicate their treatments of the subject.

It is sufficient to say that college counseling is a skilled profession, the members of which are prepared through graduate training, including supervised clinical experience. Some of the advising functions in a college, such as providing academic information, offering suggestions of courses and curricula to be taken, extending personal friendly advice, and listening sympathetically may be performed by lesser trained staff members. In a crucial matter such as personality adjustment and its influence on success or failure in college, only trained personnel are encouraged to work with students. This chapter deals solely with this highly skilled aspect of counseling.

The principles of counseling disabled students are the same principles which govern all counseling. Human personality and the techniques of working with it are not changed in a qualitative sense by the presence of a physical disability. Disabled persons have problems, some of which concern their physical disabilities. However, it is not always the disability that is the problem. It is more often the person who has the disability. This person, whose personality is a product of his total life development, may be facing serious difficulties in his adjustment. In some instances, the disability may play a major role in the problem configuration. In others, it may not. As a result, counseling the handicapped student is similar to counseling all other students. The only real difference is that the presence of a severe physical disability may introduce some points of emphasis into the counseling process which are commonly less evident in working with nondisabled students. A few of the reasons for this are discussed below:

Disabled students, as a group, probably have a greater incidence of adjustment problems than nondisabled students. This statement is based on the conclusions arrived at by Barker and associates [4] after reviewing the available research studies in this field. Thus it may be hypothesized that disabled students will use counseling help more frequently than others.

Many disabled students have been reared in family environments in which the presence of the disability has been a dynamic factor in formulating parental attitudes. Studies of disabled children reveal that parents of these children tend to find it difficult to provide the warmth and acceptance so necessary in effective child-rearing. As a result, the incidence of both overprotection and rejection is likely to be significant. According to Somers and others [4, 65], these parental attitudes tend to influence the child's adjustment. Undoubtedly, some of these attitudes accompany disabled students into their college careers and serve as deterrents to happy and successful living. For this reason, "maturing" problems are likely to be a focus in counseling these students.

Some disabilities set up barriers to personal satisfaction. As described by Barker and others [4, 21, 65], disabilities may be seen as "impermeable" membranes through which the disabled person is unlikely to pass. Furthermore, the barrier that is his disability is usually permanent and omnipresent. The constant struggle to overcome this barrier may lower the individual's frustration tolerance and make him overly sensitive to a wide variety of frustrating stimuli and their equivalents. Sometimes this results in unreal levels of aspiration which may inhibit adjustment to college, and require counseling.

The college environment may include individuals who are fearful, suspicious, and guilty where physical disability is concerned. These persons may respond to the disabled student negatively [15, 25]. One or more such encounters with faculty members, other students, and members of the administrative staff may evoke severe emotional reactions. Feelings of depression, hostility, aggressiveness, and discouragement may be generated. The disabled student may become confused and disheartened as the lack of acceptance is made obvious. At times like these he will need the services of a professional counselor.

Owing to an absence of reality-testing experiences, the disabled student may find his self-concept incongruent with the concept of him held by those around him. If there is a marked distortion in the disabled student's self-concept it may have its roots in parental attitudes toward him, the effects of segregated education, the lack of opportunities to compete and work with nondisabled persons, and the misguided "kindness" of some persons who have exaggerated his achievements in order to "be good to him." When the college environment begins to present evidence that his self-concept is at variance with the consensus, the disabled student is likely to become confused and resentful. He will probably need counseling help to understand the dynamics of his situation and to orient himself to the reality experiences he is currently having. Thus, the college counseling of the physically hand-icapped student often deals with incongruities of this type and assists the student to resolve them through reorganizing his feelings about himself.

Some disabled students have been schooled in dependency whereas the college environment places a premium on independent thought and initiative. Thrust suddenly into such an environment, the handicapped student may be temporarily unable to cope with these new expectations. His immediate need may be for a sympathetic person with whom he can develop a relationship that is initially dependent, but who will use this relationship professionally to promote the student's growth and ultimate independence. Unless this is done, the disabled student who has developed a style of life marked by dependency may find the college environment too demanding, or he may form dependency relationships with other students and exploit them to perpetuate his own dependency. A common manifestation of this feeling is the demands made on the counselor and the college. For some of these students, the college can never do enough. They constantly find inadequacies in college provisions for them and request adjustment after adjustment in their programs.

Among the continuing health problems of some disabled students may be diabetes, epilepsy, progressive losses of vision and hearing, cardiac difficulties, weakness, pain, discomfort, and the like. Often, these are primarily medical in character. The college physician has the responsibility of ascertaining the physical nature of the problem and suggesting needed remedial measures. The counselor helps to reinforce the physician, especially when the physical symptoms are accentuated by adjustment problems. In cooperation with the doctor, the counselor may help the student attain better levels of functioning through working with him on the emotional components of these problems. In any event, more commonly than with other students, the focus of counseling the disabled student is on health and related problems.

These are some of the points to be considered in offering counseling service to disabled students. Numerous other points of emphasis have been suggested by writers in the field. While it is questionable whether groups of nondisabled students can do without counseling service, disabled students, as a group, require it. The special circumstances of a severe physical limitation, living with it, and being exposed to the attitudes found in the human environment, with all their inconsistency and variability, make counseling services a necessity for disabled students. At times, the emotional situation in which the disabled person finds himself is so intense that he may require the professional help of counselors, psychologists, or social workers which almost invariably includes counseling. Sometimes this help is of a short-term nature. At other times, it requires lengthy periods of counseling. In either case, it is frequently a prerequisite to eventual self-sufficiency.

COUNSELING PROBLEMS

Despite certain differences in theoretical positions, there is much agreement among counselors of all persuasions. The areas of agreement and disagreement pertain to disabled counselees as well as to all other persons. The presence of a disability does not create qualitative changes in the person which demand special approaches. There is no "psychology of the disabled." Consequently, there is no special counseling approach to the disabled student. The counselor with a client-centered orientation should find no reason to modify this because he is working with a disabled student. The same can be said for counselors with psychoanalytic, clinical, directive, or any other type of counseling approach. The counselor merely uses the same methods with students having a physical handicap as with his other clients.

This similarity should not obscure the fact that the counselee does have a disability which has influenced his personality development and continues to be an important factor in his life. These differences are real and significant. Although they do not influence the counselor's basic techniques, they do require him to give special consideration to aspects of the client's problem which would probably receive less emphasis in working with nondisabled students. Some of these points of emphasis are discussed below:

Medical Information

Some counseling orientations minimize the use of background information. In working with a disabled student, such information is vital to an understanding of the student's problem for a number of reasons.

The disability may be a determinant of student behavior. Thus, certain neurological disabilities may result in perceptual problems. The lack of visual or hearing experiences may be manifested in misinterpretations of environmental cues. If the counselor is not aware of these variables, he may be less able to assist the student toward self-understanding and improved techniques of living.

The counselor often has the responsibility of interpreting the student's emotional reactions to the college physician, the administration, and the faculty. Some counseling orientations may deny that this is an essential role of the college counselor. However, by reason of his special insights and skills, he is often the best-equipped person on the staff to perform this function. If he fails to do it, it may not get done. On the other hand, some would argue that this is an administrative responsibility and is inconsistent with the counseling role. To some extent, this is true. However, it is difficult to see how the counselor can avoid certain administrative responsibilities in relation to the physically disabled student. These responsibilities often include participating in admissions decisions, serving on committees working on the problems of physically disabled students, helping disabled students to accept and work with college faculty members, students, and administrative officers, and interpreting the problems of the disabled student to members of the college community.

College service for the physically handicapped student requires close teamwork between the physician and the counselor. In order that each may achieve a high degree of effectiveness, there must be constant communication between them. Not infrequently, medical decisions have a bearing on the future course of a student's college career. In informing the student of findings and recommendations, the physician cannot always adopt counseling attitudes and responsibilities. It is the counselor who provides the student with opportunities to discuss his feelings about the medical data and assists him to use the information constructively. Since a good many of the handicapped student's problems center around medical limitations, treatment, and prognosis, the counselor may be of optimum service when he obtains the data from the physician and counsels the student within the framework of the medical reality.

In counseling disabled students, the physical condition often becomes the figure and the college demands serve as the background. Students use a variety of techniques to manage their feelings about their health. These run the gamut of the so-called defense mechanisms. They repress, compensate, rationalize, sublimate, and all the rest, but the disability continues to play an important role in the life of the severely disabled individual. Time and again it reappears as a dynamic in current problems and long-range attitudes. To the degree that it does, it is helpful if the counselor will work with the student with the purpose of enabling him to face the reality of his limitations. Knowing the details of the condition and the relationship between the physician and the student adds to the counselor's effectiveness in performing this function.

It is exceedingly rewarding when the counselor and the physician maintain mutual understanding and respect. Often, the training and experience of counselors and physicians serve as barriers to this happy situation. Some of the physician's attitudes which may influence the relationship are his use of authority, his unwillingness to share certain types of data, his desire to retain a counseling role himself, his wariness of psychologically oriented personnel, and his distrust of counseling as a scientific tool. On the other hand, the counselor may be inhibited in relating to the physician because of his feeling that the counseling role should be largely reserved for trained counselors, his naïveté about medical terms and problems, his demands for more detailed information than the physician can give, especially in the area of prognosis, and his possible envy of the status of the physician in our society. Obviously not all these factors enter into every relationship between a physician and a college counselor. In some cases, perhaps none of them is significant. However, when they are present walls of misunderstanding may arise between the two professions that impair service to students.

It is essential that the differentiated roles of the physician and the counselor should be clearly recognized. Sometimes, over a long period of working together, well-defined lines of function may emerge. More often, a formal attempt must be made to spell out the contributions of each. It is helpful if the administration of the institution participates in such discussions and guides them. There are some areas that are clearly medical, others that are clearly counseling. The gray areas in between form potential sources of conflict and misunderstanding.

Some physicians have not had much experience in working with counselors, and vice versa. Often, there is need for a period of mutual education. Unless this occurs and the lines are sharply drawn in the minds of the professional personnel, there is likely to be confusion on the part of the student. Together the physician and the counselor can perform the following vital tasks relating to the health problems of disabled students:

Help the student to obtain a better understanding of his medical condition and how it is affecting his performance.

Assist the student to accept his disability and to place it in proper focus, without having to deny it or elaborate upon it.

Work with the student toward accepting necessary medical treatments, precautions, and supervision.

Help the student to use rehabilitation resources which he may not yet have explored.

Assist the faculty and the administration to adopt realistic attitudes toward the disability. This may be done through example, through education, and through precept.

Sharing Responsibility with Other Agencies

Typically, disabled students receive counseling service prior to admission to college. Quite frequently, this service continues while the student is attending college. Many of these students are sponsored by a state rehabilitation agency, and usually an agency counselor continues to give counseling service through the college years. Or staff members of social agencies, rehabilitation centers, hospitals, and other organizations may be following the student. Each may perceive himself as having a role in counseling the student. Unless these counseling services are properly organized, with a differentiation of function, the student may be overwhelmed with overlapping counseling and confused by varying orientations and emphases. The college counselor often assumes responsibility for coordinating these various efforts. Distribution of these efforts may result in the rehabilitation counselor taking responsibility for problems of a vocational nature while the college counselor works with problems arising in the academic and social areas. If other types of counselors are participating, similar arrangements are usually developed.

Since emotional problems permeate all areas of counseling, the depth of service offered by the college counselor to the disabled student varies with the policy of the institution, the competence of the counselor, and the extent of other counseling. If the disabled student is receiving case-work assistance or psychotherapy, the college counselor will probably function on a more superficial level, limiting his service to supportive and informational roles. This same problem is encountered among nondisabled students, but is more likely to occur with the handicapped group because, coincident with their college experience, many of these students are involved in other educational and rehabilitative processes.

Assessment

A major goal of counseling is to enable the counselee to become better informed about his capacities and limitations. This is especially crucial with some handicapped students who, when they enter higher education, have had limited experience in testing themselves against the norms of the general population. This initial period of self-discovery in the first year of college can be difficult for students coming from sheltered or semi-sheltered environments. Some disabled students may find themselves compared with a select group of nondisabled persons, with results less favorable than they had expected. They may be completely unprepared for their new status. Something of the same sort happens to a number of nondisabled students who, after having held lofty positions in their community schools, discover that they are only average in the new learning situation of the college.

In some cases, the initial assessment of academic achievement may not be entirely valid. Transition from the secondary school with its special provisions to the college campus with its minimal modifications may catch the student unprepared. Compelled to use tools of communication more intensively than ever before, and to meet physical demands that are greater than expected, the disabled student may face many problems in his freshman year. During this period of adjustment, his academic performance may fall below his potentialities. He may need a relatively lengthy period to adapt himself to the new conditions. Once having done so, usually through testing various techniques of study and reading, the disabled student may rise gradually to a higher level of performance.

The high school grades of disabled students are sometimes open to doubt. Students educated through home instruction tend to have inflated grades. To some extent, this is true of students who have spent part or all of their secondary school years in special classes or schools. The smaller size of these classes, the specialized methods and materials used, and the norms used tend to give grades which exaggerate the actual attainment. In assessing a student's high school grades, the counselor should look beyond the grade to the individual who did the grading, for only in this way can the counselor make assumptions about the representativeness of the grade. Some instructors, moved by emotion, will not fail handicapped students or give them low grades, rationalizing their action on the basis of—"He has enough to cope with without my giving him low grades."

College counselors often use standardized tests to help students increase their self-knowledge. Many tests can be used with severely disabled students without hesitation; others require specialized techniques and approaches. It is important that the counselor be able to answer the following questions in using test results pertaining to severely disabled students:

Is the test valid for a person with this limitation?   Many apparatus tests measure quite different aptitudes for blind persons than for seeing. For example, the Minnesota Rate of Manipulation Test tends to measure space orientation as much as gross manual dexterity when administered to students without vision. Intelligence tests using language tend to measure the language aspects of intelligence rather than the global concept when used with deaf students who may be language handicapped. Some performance tests, such as the Blocks Subtest of the Wechsler Adult Intelligence Scale, measure the impaired perception of some cerebral palsied students rather the intelligent manipulation of materials, pictures, and ideas.

Are the norms comparable?   Most tests are scored on the basis of comparing the performance of the testee with the performance of others who are similar to him. Presence of a severe physical limitation may reduce the assumption of comparability to such a degree that confidence in the printed norms will be limited.

Does the disability have elements which will influence test performance so as to becloud the meanings of the scores? For example, some disabilities of the nervous system tend to affect perception and speed of response. Scores on tests which require speed and sharpness of perception will be greatly influenced by the student's physical condition. If a hearing handicapped individual is unable to fully understand the instructions given to him by the examiner his test scores may be understated.

Are the test items within the disabled student's experience? Some tests penalize congenitally blind and deaf students by including items which subsume previous visual and aural experiences. Other test items are built on the assumption that the individual has had a normal family experience. Yet a number of severely disabled college students have spent much of their lives in hospitals, convalescent homes, and institutions.

Counselors should also know whether the test was properly challenging to the disabled student, whether he was motivated to work with the problems presented, and whether the disability made it necessary to modify the administration of the test. The problems involved in using standardized tests for assessment of severely disabled students may become so complex that the typical college counselor will require expert assistance from clinical and counseling psychologists who have had experience in working with members of various disability groups. Their participation in the assessment procedures will contribute to an adequate evaluation.

Tests, ratings, grades, and observations all contribute to a better understanding of the disabled student and have value as techniques which require relatively short periods of time. However, in service to disabled children and adults, it has been found that these approaches are most effective when supplemented by work samples or on-the-job evaluations. Under a work sample scheme, the disabled person is given a series of tasks which are replicas of life situations. Over a period of weeks or months, he learns the tasks and performs them in realistic settings, often in workshops and rehabilitation centers. During this period, the disabled individual is observed, counseled, and instructed. Daily recordings note his attitudes and behavior. As the work trial progresses, the environment is adjusted to meet his needs and to present new and more demanding challenges to him. Although this technique has been found helpful with disabled adolescents and adults in industrial settings, it is difficult to see its applicability in an educational institution. College life is so complex that the selection of a few tasks and the exposure of the student to a few more or less artificial situations may not truly reflect his ultimate performance.

On-the-job evaluation seems more appropriate for a college or university. Under this arrangement, the student attends the institution for a trial period. A summer session would probably be the easiest to arrange, although one of the regular semesters or quarters might do just as well. The student is aware of the fact that this is an assessment as well as a learning experience for him. During the trial period, he is exposed to a variety of experiences. He may be asked to take two or more courses of varied character, demanding different abilities. He is assigned to a dormitory, enrolled in activities of his own choice, given periodic counseling interviews, asked to see the physician at different points in the trial period, and is interviewed at least once or twice by members of the college administration. Each staff member who comes in contact with the student during this period is asked to make notes on his observations of the student's capacity to work within the college framework. Unless serious adjustment problems occur, the disabled student is permitted to complete the trial period. When all the reports have been analyzed a comprehensive report is prepared and submitted to the administration. On the basis of this report and other available data, decisions are made about the student. Often, the counselor serves as coordinator of the student's program and is responsible for the collection of data.

This rather extensive procedure is neither necessary nor desirable for most disabled students. There may be a small number whose disabilities are so pervasive and severe and whose emotional problems are so serious as to raise doubts about their attendance despite satisfactory performance in the secondary school, and, perhaps, in college. Under these circumstances, in fairness to the student and to the institution, an on-the-job assessment has the advantage of trying the student out in a real setting. The results of such an assessment do not require extrapolation. They are the products of a real experience under conditions almost identical with those the disabled student will face in the college over the long term. Thus, they have a relevancy and an immediacy which are quite compelling.

Problems of the Counselor

As a group, college counselors are likely to have had limited experience with severely disabled students. Their ability to accept disabled students and to work with them with a minimum of emotional involvement may be assumed in view of their choice of counseling as a career and their professional training. Yet counselors, like others in our society, are subject to a wide range of attitudes toward disability. Some of these attitudes are healthy, conducive to the formation of a professional counseling relationship. Others may impair the development of a good relationship with the student and subsequent service to him.

The counselor may have vague misgivings about working with certain students, or he may feel inadequate in counseling them, or be subject to anxiety in their presence. When he has such feelings, he should discuss them with his supervisor. This course of action helps the counselor to understand what is happening and enables him to continue working with students whose limitations, appearance, or dependency disturb him. If good supervision is not available to the counselor, or if he is unable to profit from it, it would be advisable to transfer the disabled student to another counselor, if this is possible.

Consultation with Parents

All college counselors do some work in parent consultation. It is almost inevitable that contacts with parents of disabled students will be more frequent than with parents of nondisabled students. Some parents are quite anxious about their disabled children in the college environment. There is no way to predict the many complex motivations that bring them to the counselor. Among the elements which may intensify their anxiety about their children are real concern as to their capacity to function in the more demanding college setting, guilt growing out of their negative feelings toward their children, a sense of responsibility for having made their children unduly dependent on them, a need to have their children succeed to justify all the efforts and sacrifices which have been made, and countless others.

A common focus of student-parent conflict is independence. Often the disabled student sees college as an opportunity to lessen dependency relationships with his family and to learn to live in a more emancipated fashion. This may be resisted by the parents who will resent his failure to correspond with them as often as they believe he should, his less frequent calls for help, his development of new relationships at college which make him less dependent on them, and his attempts to do more for himself. Parents may come to the counselor for an explanation of this behavior. They may even see in him a person who is attempting to set himself up as a parent surrogate. Other problems that parents may present are questions about the student's performance, concern about his health, requests for special privileges, and attempts to provide the counselor with data about the student which they believe he should have.

Actually, the parent consultation given is relatively superficial. If the counselor is to retain a healthy counseling relationship with the disabled student, it is important for him to keep the student informed about interviews with his parents. He should tell the student that the college expects him to see parents when they request it, but assure him that all that has passed between them in the counseling situation will continue to be confidential. In addition, the counselor should tell the parent at the beginning of the interview that he may have to share some of the content of this interview with the student.

During the course of parent consultation, the counselor does not reveal any confidential information. He is able to share with the parents student grades, reports, and progress as these appear in publicly released form. He may also make some generalized statements about the student's progress and prospects. By far the major function is that of giving parents an opportunity to ventilate feelings. It is also a chance for the counselor to learn about the student-parent relationship as the parent sees it. In addition, he can give the parent some reassurance that the student is receiving service at the college and that his needs are recognized.

At times, the parent may ask for personal help. He may feel

uncomfortable in his relationship with his child, and may ask the counselor to help him to a better understanding of the situation. It should remain clear throughout that the student is the client, not the parent. The counselor cannot assume the role of professional counselor to the parent. The best that he can do is to share certain relatively superficial materials with him and suggest community resources to which the parent may turn.

Working with the Faculty

Some faculty members may need help in working with severely disabled students. Many faculty-student problems can be forestalled if the faculty members are provided with basic data about the student. In doing this, the counselor must avoid revealing confidential information, which is not always easy. Staff members may feel that they have a right to information concerning a student's disability and his special problems. Some fear that they may ask the student to perform activities which are contraindicated by his disability in terms of safety and capacity. Others feel that they can do a more effective teaching job when they know their students well enough to individualize instruction. Still others are insecure in their work with disabled students. Each bit of additional information which they have tends to add to their perceived security in the situation.

In actuality, sound educational practice requires that some data be shared with faculty members. Their attitudes toward these students may be aided by such data, they will be enabled to key their instruction better to student needs, and they will have a greater sense of participation in the program serving disabled students. The question is: What kinds of information can be released and how much of it?

As part of its total policy relating to severely disabled students, the institution should clearly indicate the types of data which must be placed at the disposal of teachers. This should be discussed with the disabled student prior to his admission and, if possible, a signed release should be obtained from him, countersigned by his parents. At the beginning of each semester short statements should be distributed to faculty members; these statements contain the basic minimum data stipulated by the college policy in regard to severely disabled students.

It is seldom necessary to reveal the medical diagnosis or prognosis of the student or to use medical terminology. The statement should simply and briefly report the elemental facts which bear on classroom performance. The following examples are paraphrased from the records of one institution which has adopted this procedure:

Mr. T. has a physical condition which is not discernible to the observer. He is capable of performing all academic requirements in your course, but he should not be asked to walk up and down steps, run, move furniture, carry more than a few books, or exert himself physically in any way. If there is any evidence of fatigue, unusual difficulty in breathing, or lassitude, it is suggested that you notify the Medical Office as a precaution. This student is known to the Counseling Service. If he presents any unusual academic or social problems, a member of the Counseling Service staff would be glad to discuss him with you.

Miss J. has impaired vision. She wears corrective lenses, but even with this assistance, there are certain visual activities which are beyond her capacities. She can see the blackboard, illustrations, films, etc., in good light from a distance no greater than 3 feet. The fluorescent lights in your room will be helpful to her even on days when there is usually enough daylight so that you would not ordinarily turn on the lights. She is accustomed to sitting in the front row as close as possible to the place from which you teach. This enables her to see your face more clearly and to catch some of the subtleties of your expression. Her vision is good enough for her to take her own notes in black pencil on unruled paper. She can also take essay examinations without special help through using a magnifying glass which she carries with her. However, reading materials for periods over a quarter of an hour tend to result in physical symptoms which lessen her efficiency. If you give quizzes or objective tests which require more than fifteen minutes of reading, she should be given two days' notice or more so that she can arrange to hire someone to read the material to her. Very soon after the beginning of the term, Miss J. will discuss the qualifications of several readers with you. You may accept or reject any of them. She will be permitted to take such tests in the Counseling Service under the supervision of one of the secretaries who has had some experience in making these arrangements. Miss J. will have many of your assignments read to her. However, she has had considerable experience in doing this and expects to meet all the requirements of your course. You should expect her to complete all the work assigned to the class. If you have any questions about this student, you may wish to discuss them with the college physician or the college counselor. Both will be happy to confer with you at your convenience.

At least three individuals should participate in preparing these statements. The college physician and the college counselor should prepare the initial statement, making certain that it is accurate in all details and that it does not reveal confidential information other than that demanded by college policy. It should then be discussed with the student. Quite often, he will be able to add to it so that its content will be more helpful to the instructor. At the very least, he should be aware of the contents of this communication and prepared to discuss it with the instructor if the need should arise.

There are other kinds of problems concerning physically handicapped students which require counselor contacts with faculty members. In most cases, these problems are similar to those which faculty members have with other students. They include underachievement, atypical classroom behavior, examination performance, relationships with other students in class, requests for special considerations, and attitudes toward the disability. The major difference is that the teacher is likely to see the disability as a determinant of the problem behavior. When this is so, and within the bounds of confidentiality, the counselor attempts to help the staff member to understand the limitations of the student and suggests techniques for working with him. In most cases, the atypical behavior that is disturbing to the instructor is only remotely related to the disability. The counselor can help the faculty member to view the disability in perspective, as only one dynamic in the life of the student. Some instructors are inclined to see the limitations as all-encompassing. In effect, the student becomes overdrawn as the possessor of a disability rather than as a person who is multifaceted, as we all are, with the disability playing only a part in his development.

Some faculty members are greatly disturbed when they find a severely disabled student in their classes, and have actually requested his removal, claiming that he is distracting the group. The feelings of the instructor may be so deeply rooted that the usual informational methods are of little help. Such instructors may react so strongly to the presence of certain disabled students, and may be so resistant to attempts to ease the problem, that the only alternative is to transfer the student to another class, if this is possible. Usually, however, over-reactions of faculty members stem from lack of experience with and information about such students. After conferences with the counselor and favorable contacts with the students, many instructors alter their perceptions of these students and become relatively skillful in working with them. They may even become converts to the principles of educating severely disabled college students and active sponsors of plans to expand the service.

Although the college counselor does not play a counseling role with faculty members any more than with parents, he can give them certain types of information about the physically handicapped students. The counselor can also provide faculty members with an opportunity to express their feelings. Some instructors have highly personalized feelings about certain disabilities, but after ventilating them, they may feel more positively about their responsibilities to students with marked physical limitations. Finally, the counselor can suggest mechanics which may assist the teacher and the student to work together more smoothly. These suggestions are usually simple ideas which facilitate classroom organization and management as they concern the disabled student. They may include problems of seating, early dismissal from class, standards that should be set for the student, the degree of verbal participation to be required of him, the amount of individualized attention he should receive, other special provisions that should be made, and the techniques of handling the feelings of other students toward the disability.

Given this level of help, most faculty members soon become fully independent in their relationships with severely disabled students. If the counselor can help them to see the realities of the disability, as well as the essential intellectual and emotional normalcy of these handicapped students, it will contribute to the well-being of all the students in the institution.

SPECIAL CONSIDERATIONS IN SELECTING TECHNIQUES

Counseling the physically disabled student is a process undertaken with a human being who, despite even the most evident of physical differences, is fundamentally like other human beings. Unique approaches and basic modifications in counseling technique are not required. Assisted by some specialized knowledge and employing points of consideration and emphasis noted earlier, the counselor may expect to work successfully with disabled students. At times, he may need consultative help from specialists and supervision, but the counseling orientation which he finds effective with all clients should be equally effective with physically handicapped college students.

"Schools" of counseling differ from each other to some degree. Current evidence does not suggest that one approach is markedly superior to any other in counseling disabled students. Among the hallmarks of effective counseling which apply equally to this group are development of a good professional relationship, provision of opportunities to express feelings, emphasis on client activity in the clarification of problems, essentiality of client learning in the counseling experience, movement of clients from negative to positive feelings and ideas, growth in self-awareness, increasing ability of clients to take responsibility for their own lives, improvement in independent decision-making capacity, and, ultimately, growing independence from the counselor and ability to go on without his continuing support. All these are ingredients in counseling disabled college students. However, the nature of the disability and its impact on the student may demand certain special considerations and adaptations of technique.

Communication Problems

Some disabilities such as sensory limitations, speech problems, perceptual disorders, and paucity of life experiences may impair the free verbal communication that plays an important role in counseling. In interviewing disabled students, counselors must be constantly aware of possible problems in communication and ready to make the needed adaptations. Some deaf students, lacking speech, may have to communicate through writing. In doing so, they may reveal language limitations which affect their ability to express feelings and concepts in words. An orthopedically handicapped student who has spent the greater part of his life in hospitals under an authoritarian structure may have some difficulty in perceiving the counselor in nonauthoritarian terms, in the beginning, and in communicating with him on such terms. Obviously, problems of communication concern all counselors with all clients. With disabled students, it is an area which frequently requires special consideration.

New Situations and Overlapping Situations

Barker and his associates, in describing a somatopsychological approach to understanding the problems of handicapped persons, stress the special emotional difficulties encountered by such persons when they enter unfamiliar social situations. Counseling experience confirms that these are areas of sensitivity to many physically disabled individuals. Some physically handicapped students encounter adjustment problems when they become involved in any life situation which has the properties of "newness." Similarly, especially among those who are only partially disabled or who have "hidden" handicaps (such as diabetes, cardiovascular difficulties, and the like), some tension is likely to focus around the problem of deciding whether to conceal or reveal the physical disability. Problems of status, of minority group feelings, and of coping with the inconsistent and partially unpredictable attitudes toward disability in our culture may be dynamics in the current life problems of disabled students. Yet these constitute only a part of the special problems of living with a disability.

The somatopsychological focus on new and overlapping situations has been selected as illustrating a more general problem. In certain respects, a severe physical handicap constitutes a barrier to the ready satisfaction of some life goals, and as such it demands special investigation and study. Summaries of this type of work may be found in *Adjustment to Physical Handicap and Illness* by R. G. Barker and others (New York: Social Science Research Council, 1956), and in *Psychology of Exceptional Children and Youth,* edited by W. M. Cruickshank (Englewood Cliffs, N. J.: Prentice-Hall, Inc., 1955). Many colleges and universities providing preparation in special education and rehabilitation counseling offer one or more courses in the psychological aspects of physical disability. Counselors for disabled students will perform more effectively if they keep themselves informed in this area in which a body of knowledge has now been developed, some of it bearing on the counseling process.

ISSUES IN THE ADMINISTRATION OF COLLEGE COUNSELING PROGRAMS

An attempt was made earlier in this chapter to suggest the importance of a counseling program for the physically disabled college student. Perhaps it is even more important for him than for other students. However, it is difficult to maintain effective student personnel services for disabled students without doing so for nondisabled students. Thus, the approach in this volume is not one of providing segregated services within a special department or area of the institution. On the contrary, services to disabled students are perceived as one aspect in the provision of services to all students. The reasons for this approach will become clear as the problems involved in administering a counseling program for disabled students are discussed.

Differentiation from the General Counseling Program

A few colleges and universities have established comprehensive student personnel programs for disabled students. For example, City College in New York has assigned a full-time counselor to work with disabled students, and for a number of years, Hunter College in New York assigned a part-time counselor to this function. A more elaborate program is one which has been in operation for more than ten years at the Student Rehabilitation Center of the University of Illinois. As the coordinating campus agency for students with severe physical handicaps, this Center offers a broad spectrum of services.

In addition to providing counseling and physical therapy, the program influences planning throughout the institution. It is reported that progress has been achieved in making campus and classrooms more accessible through ramps and elevators. Southern Illinois University is a second example of an institution with comprehensive on-campus services for handicapped students.

These ambitious programs are exceedingly valuable. They make attendance at courses possible for some severely disabled students who otherwise might be denied educational opportunities at higher levels. In addition, they serve as demonstration centers, pioneering in the use of new approaches and techniques. Observing their work and benefiting from their experience, professional workers adapt their findings to local situations. Furthermore, these centers are valuable sources for research in this area. However, for most colleges and universities, in terms of numbers of disabled students and financial and personnel resources available, more modest approaches are appropriate.

In organizing such a modest counseling program for physically disabled students, the institution may move in either of two directions—toward differentiation or integration. At the outset, it must be acknowledged that a small number of very severely disabled students will require intensive and continuing counseling service. If these students are accepted for admission, the institution may have to adopt a differentiated approach. As a minimum, a professional person with specialized interests and training should be assigned the counseling function, or easy access to professional rehabilitation consultation should be available. Without this assistance, the severely disabled student may lack the counseling and coordinating services that are essential for his successful achievement in college. However, the number of students requiring this assistance, although currently specifically unascertainable, is quite small.

A college or university may find it reasonable and economical to make these resources accessible to other less severely handicapped students. Thus, the institution may move toward a differentiated program for many of its physically limited students. This differentiation may be manifested in a special counselor for the disabled, special quarters and study facilities for them, and an administrative unit designed to facilitate the organization and functioning of the program.

Other institutions have adopted integration. They have avoided a special administrative unit for disabled students, the assignment of special personnel on a full- or long-term basis to these students, and the designation of the group as a special caseload. These institutions have attempted to weave all but the most severely disabled students into the regular program, assigning them for counseling to general counselors available for all students. Every attempt is made to serve them through existing facilities. Only where absolutely necessary are special provisions of facilities and personnel made. Wherever possible, the welfare of the disabled student becomes the concern and responsibility of the whole college staff, although one or more persons may be given coordinating roles.

Insofar as physical limitations permit, the second approach seems to have certain advantages. It is consistent with the current philosophy that disabled persons, in most respects, can be integrated into existing structures. It is in keeping with the desires of many less severely disabled students who resist segregation and what they consider to be subsequent stigmatization. It assists in educating the total staff. Finally, it places responsibility for the disabled student in the institution, as a whole, rather than in the hands of a few specialists.

Contrariwise, several disadvantages should be recorded. This approach may not work with a small minority of extremely disabled persons who require differentiated services. It may be less efficient in that less well-trained personnel will become more deeply involved in the program. In an institution in which leadership and participation by key personnel are lacking, the disabled student may actually suffer neglect or avoidance. In reality, integration and differentiation in student personnel services are extremes. Most institutions develop patterns that lie somewhere along a continuum. In most instances, integration is viewed as a desirable ideal to be pursued, and practiced whenever possible. The greater the number of severely disabled students accepted for admission, the more extensive will be the need for differentiated organizational structures. However, even when this differentiation becomes necessary, it is advisable to keep it from "spilling over" into the ranks of the less severely disabled students. Despite the presence of highly organized services for severely handicapped students, those who can do so should be encouraged to use the general counseling services and to become integrated into the ordinary academic and social life of the college.

Aggressive Case-Finding vs. Self-Referral

Some institutions provide counseling services which participate in identifying, admitting, and orienting new disabled students. Subsequent to this initial service, they maintain a caseload of such students. If the members of this caseload, whether they feel they need it or not, fail to appear voluntarily at the counseling office, they will be invited periodically to see the counselor. Other institutions provide counseling only when referrals are made by college personnel or other agencies, or in the case of self-referrals by the student. It is their feeling that routine follow-up contacts achieve very limited goals. In view of these varying approaches, how aggressive should a counseling service be in calling in physically disabled students who are not referred and do not apply voluntarily for counseling?

Student personnel services need to take the initiative in certain aspects of their programs. For example, periodic medical examinations must be conducted, whether or not the student asks for them. Programs must be planned in advance in order to make curriculum and other adjustments which may be necessary. Periodic reviews of grades may be required to prepare reports for state rehabilitation agencies. In each of these instances, the counselor may take the initiative in arranging a conference with the student.

When the needs are not administrative, the question of initiative takes on a different meaning. Disabled students have as much right and responsibility in entering or not entering counseling as any other students. The acceptance of nonadministrative counseling should be based, as it is for all students, on the perceptions of the individual. If the student sees a need for counseling and is ready to accept it from a college source, then counseling is appropriate for him. On the other hand, if the counseling does not develop from administrative requirements, the student has the prerogative of accepting counseling from the college, from other sources, or not at all. Disability in itself does not introduce any special compulsion into the situation. The nonadministrative counseling needs of the disabled student should be handled in precisely the same way as similar needs of nondisabled students.

Looking at it from another point of view, the counselor of the physically disabled student has, by necessity, certain administrative responsibilities. Although the disabled student participates in fulfilling these responsibilities, he must accept the demands of the situation. If periodic physical examinations are required, he must meet this requirement in order to remain in college. If preliminary program planning is required, he must participate in that, too. However, if most students in the institution are free to accept or reject nonadministrative counseling, the disabled student should have the same freedom of choice.

In this chapter, a number of administrative problems that may arise in counseling physically disabled students have been discussed. Sometimes the disabled student needs more counseling, the counseling may have additional emphases, and it may demand an understanding of psychological aspects of physical disability. With the exception of unusually severely disabled students, most of these needs can be met within the framework of an existing counseling service. In fact, this type of arrangement assists the student to become better integrated into the life of the college or university.

Resources Available for Personnel Workers Serving Physically Handicapped College Students

6

THE PROBLEMS of severe physical disability are often so complex that a single agency cannot meet all or even the greater part of a college student's needs. A disability may have medical, psychological, educational, social, and vocational aspects. Even a highly organized comprehensive rehabilitation center may find that external services are needed. The college performs its function, but at best this concerns only one aspect of the student's total problem. Other agencies are needed and are sometimes available to provide complementary services. As part of their training, college personnel workers are prepared to develop and maintain cooperative relationships with community agencies. The techniques of achieving this will not be discussed in this chapter.

There is a multiplicity of these community resources. Agencies for the physically disabled function on national, state, and local levels, and are either publicly or privately supported. Problems of physical disability have been widely recognized and have led to broad legislation as well as to extensive private philanthropic efforts on their behalf. Only a brief list of major organizations will be presented in this volume. Each counselor can supplement it by a survey of the local and state groups most active in the community he serves.

LOCAL AND STATE AGENCIES

The major types of local and state agencies for the disabled are described below.

Rehabilitation Centers

The rehabilitation center offers a comprehensive rehabilitation program, usually with a medical and/or vocational focus. Among the types of services offered are medical, physical, occupational, and speech therapy; clinical and counseling psychology; nursing; recreation and group work; social casework; vocational counseling, evaluation, and training; vocational placement; and others. Usually, these are housed in a single facility, and the patient or client may receive all or part of his rehabilitation service here. As a rule, other agencies participate in the work of the center. There are a few state-supported public rehabilitation centers, but most of them are local or regional in character, and derive at least some of their funds from private sources. A listing of rehabilitation centers may be obtained from The Conference of Rehabilitation Centers and Facilities, 928 Davis Street, Evanston, Illinois.

State Rehabilitation Agencies

Functioning under federal and state legislation, rehabilitation agencies provide public tax-supported services to disabled persons within a particular state or territory. A majority of states have two state rehabilitation agencies—one for the blind and one for persons with other disabilities. About one-fourth of the states have a single agency serving both blind and nonblind persons. At present, the services of these agencies are available primarily to individuals whose disability constitutes an employment handicap. College students with severe physical limitations often fall into this group. There is a movement under way to serve individuals whose disabilities are so severe that employment is not the major goal but who require other types of assistance. Appropriate legislation to implement this expansion of service has been introduced into Congress.

Among the services which these state agencies offer are medical, psychological, and vocational diagnosis; physical restoration; vocational counseling; prevocational and vocational training; vocational placement; provision of employment supplies and equipment; and follow-up and research. The details of service to physically disabled college students vary from state to state. However, all these agencies are deeply interested in the problems and plans of severely disabled college students. One of the essential tasks of a college counselor working with physically handicapped students is the development of a close working relationship with the state agency or agencies concerned. A list of these agencies and their main offices is presented here.

STATE VOCATIONAL REHABILITATION AGENCIES

ALABAMA:
  416 State Office Building, Montgomery
ALASKA:
  P. O. Box 2568, Alaska Office Building, Juneau
ARIZONA:
  1704 West Adams Street, Phoenix
  *State Office Building, Room 126, Phoenix
ARKANSAS:
  303 Education Building, Little Rock
CALIFORNIA:
  721 Capitol Avenue, Sacramento
COLORADO:
  510 State Office Building, Denver
  *100 West Seventh Avenue, Denver
CONNECTICUT:
  33 Garden Street, Hartford
  *State Office Building, Hartford
DELAWARE:
  11 Concord Avenue, Wilmington
  *305–307 West Eighth Street, Wilmington
DISTRICT OF COLUMBIA:
  819–821 Ninth Street N.W., Washington, D. C.
FLORIDA:
  105 Knott Building, Tallahassee
  *P. O. Box 1229, Tampa
GEORGIA:
  129 State Office Building, Atlanta
GUAM:
  Department of Education, Agana
HAWAII:
  P. O. Box 2360, Honolulu
  *1390 Miller Street, Honolulu

* Serves blind persons exclusively.

IDAHO:
  State House, Boise
  *103 Ninth Street, Box 1189, Boise
ILLINOIS:
  400 South Spring Street, Springfield
INDIANA:
  11th Floor, 145 West Washington Street, Indianapolis
  *536 West 30th Street, Indianapolis
IOWA:
  415 Bankers Trust Building, Des Moines
  *East 12th and Court Streets, Commerce Commission Building,
    Des Moines
KANSAS:
  State Office Building, 11th Floor, Topeka
  *State Office Building, Topeka
KENTUCKY:
  State Office Building, Frankfort
LOUISIANA:
  2655 Plank Road, Baton Rouge
  *P. O. Box 4065, Baton Rouge
MAINE:
  32 Winthrop Street, Augusta
  *State House, Augusta
MARYLAND:
  2 West Redwood Street, Baltimore
MASSACHUSETTS:
  200 Newbury Street, Boston
  *90 Tremont Street, Boston
MICHIGAN:
  900 Bauch Building, Lansing
  *Fourth Floor, Lewis Cass Building, Lansing
MINNESOTA:
  301 State Office Building, St. Paul
  *117 University Avenue, St. Paul
MISSISSIPPI:
  316 Woolfolk State Office Building, P. O. Box 1698, Jackson
  *614 State Office Building, P. O. Box 1669, Jackson
MISSOURI:
  Jefferson Building, Seventh Floor, Jefferson City
  *State Office Building, Jefferson City
MONTANA:
  508 Power Block, Helena
  *10th and Ewing Streets, Helena

NEBRASKA:
State Capitol Building, 10th Floor, Lincoln
*State Capitol Building, Lincoln

NEVADA:
Room 103, Capitol Building Annex, Carson City
*State Welfare Department, P. O. Box 1331, Reno

NEW HAMPSHIRE:
State House, Concord
*State House Annex, Concord

NEW JERSEY:
38 S. Clinton Avenue, Trenton
*1100 Raymond Boulevard, Newark

NEW MEXICO:
119 South Castillo, P. O. Box 881, Santa Fe
*Department of Public Welfare, P. O. Box 1391, Santa Fe

NEW YORK:
42 North Pearl Street, Albany
*112 State Street, Albany

NORTH CAROLINA:
Department of Public Instruction, Raleigh
*Mansion Park Building, P. O. Box 2658, Raleigh

NORTH DAKOTA:
Box BB, University Station, Grand Forks

OHIO:
79 East State Street, Columbus
*85 South Washington Avenue, Columbus

OKLAHOMA:
1212 North Hudson, Oklahoma City

OREGON:
1178 Chemeketa Street, N. E., Salem
*535 S.E. 12th Avenue, Portland

PENNSYLVANIA:
Labor and Industry Building, 7th and Forster Streets, Harrisburg
*Health and Welfare Building, 7th and Forster Streets, Harrisburg

PUERTO RICO:
Stop 34½, Zequeira Building, Hato Rey

RHODE ISLAND:
205 Benefit Street, Providence
*24 Exchange Place, 7th Floor, Providence

SOUTH CAROLINA:
Room 217, 1015 Main Street, Columbia
*State Department of Public Welfare, Columbia

SOUTH DAKOTA:
   State Capitol Building, Pierre
   *New State Office Building, Pierre
TENNESSEE:
   1717 West End, Room 615, Nashville
   *303 State Office Building, Nashville
TEXAS:
   1st Floor Land Office Building, Austin
UTAH:
   400 Atlas Building, 36 West 2d South, Salt Lake City
VERMONT:
   16 Langdon Street, Montpelier
   *Department of Social Welfare, 128 State Street, Montpelier
VIRGINIA:
   State Department of Education, Richmond
   *3003 Parkwood Avenue, Richmond
VIRGIN ISLANDS:
   Vocational Rehabilitation, Charlotte Amalie, St. Thomas
WASHINGTON:
   Old Capitol Building, P. O. Box 688, Olympia
   *Department of Public Assistance, P. O. Box 1162, Olympia
WEST VIRGINIA:
   State Capitol Building, Room W–400, Charleston
WISCONSIN:
   14 North Carroll Street, Madison
   *311 State Street, Madison
WYOMING:
   123 State Capitol Building, Cheyenne

Community Counseling Agencies

Many communities are served by agencies which provide counseling services to youth and adults, disabled or not. As a result of the expansion of rehabilitation services during the past ten years, many of these agencies have developed an interest and competence in serving physically disabled individuals. In fact, some of them have established differentiated services for disabled persons through assigning specially trained counselors to work with them. In a number of cases, training centers and workshops for the disabled have been added to the usual counseling and placement services of these agencies. A list of such agencies may be found in the Directory of Vocational Counseling Services prepared by the American Board on Professional Standards in Vocational Counseling, Incorporated, and published by the American Personnel and Guidance Association, 1605 New Hampshire Avenue, N.W., Washington 9, D.C. This reference reports only on those agencies which have applied for and received a listing from the Board. There are other similar agencies which have not yet applied for or received such a listing. If a counselor desires to locate them in a community, he may inquire of the local community council, united fund, or welfare information service.

Sheltered Workshops

A sheltered workshop is a work setting in which the primary emphasis is on the provision of a paid work experience. Usually, these workshops are built around commercial and industrial work tasks. Individuals who are unable to find work for themselves because of the limitations of their disabilities, lack of training and job experience, emotional problems, lack of work tolerance, inadequate work habits and attitudes, or the lack of job opportunities are given paid employment. In many cases, this employment is temporary, depending on the development of the disabled person's ability to work, and the location of work opportunities for him. In some instances, however, this workshop experience may extend over a number of years.

The workshop may be used as a tool in the college student's rehabilitation, but he seldom turns to it for long-term employment. Some of them provide summer work opportunities for severely disabled college students in the belief that such experiences contribute to the maturity and ultimate success of the individual. Generally the workshop is part of a larger rehabilitation program and the work experience given the disabled student is likely to be part of a more comprehensive service. A list of some of the sheltered workshops may be found in the directory of the National Association of Sheltered Workshops and Homebound Programs, 1025 Vermont Avenue, Washington 5, D.C.

Specialized Local Agencies

Numerous local agencies serve persons with one or more types of disability. There are agencies for the blind, the deaf, the cerebral palsied, cardiacs, persons with multiple sclerosis, muscular dystrophy, and others. The patterns of service vary from community to community, some providing a single major service such as medical clinics or recreation, others offering multidisciplinary programs of considerable magnitude. Many of these local agencies are affiliates of larger state or national groups. One may ascertain their presence in a community through consulting the national offices of these groups. Or it may be possible to secure information from the local community council or other coordinating group, if there is one. The local office of the state rehabilitation agency is well informed about local community resources and makes its information readily available to other groups.

State Employment Services

Every state maintains a network of state employment service offices, many of which have a special interest in disabled persons. The larger units may have a special placement service for the physically handicapped, and the smaller units may assign one or more employment workers to this group. In either event, they provide vocational evaluation, placement, and counseling to disabled students. They may be helpful in counseling the disabled student relative to summer employment, part-time jobs, and the occupational outlook in his chosen field. A list of the main offices of the state employment services is presented below:

STATE EMPLOYMENT SERVICES

ALABAMA:
Department of Industrial Relations, State Office Building, Montgomery 4

ALASKA:
Employment Security Division, Department of Labor, Box 2661, Juneau

ARIZONA:
Arizona State Employment Service, 1720 West Madison Street, Phoenix

ARKANSAS:
Employment Security Division, Department of Labor, Employment Security-Welfare Building, Box 2981, Little Rock

CALIFORNIA:
Department of Employment, 800 Capitol Avenue, Sacramento 14

COLORADO:
Department of Employment, 1210 Sherman Street, Denver 3

CONNECTICUT:
Employment Security Division, Department of Labor, 92 Farmington Avenue, Hartford 15

DELAWARE:
Unemployment Compensation Commission, 601 Shipley Street, Wilmington 99

DISTRICT OF COLUMBIA:
United States Employment Service, 1724 F Street, N.W., Washington 25, D. C.

FLORIDA:
Industrial Commission, Caldwell Building, Tallahassee

GEORGIA:
Employment Security Agency, Department of Labor, State Labor Building, Atlanta 3

GUAM:
Department of Labor and Personnel, Government of Guam, Agana

HAWAII:
Department of Labor and Industrial Relations, Keelikolani Building, 825 Mililani Street, Honolulu 6

IDAHO:
Employment Security Agency, 317 Main Street, Boise

ILLINOIS:
Commissioner of Placement and Unemployment Compensation, Department of Labor, 165 North Canal Street, Chicago 6

INDIANA:
Employment Security Division, 141 South Meridian Street, Indianapolis 25

IOWA:
Employment Security Commission, 112 Eleventh Street, Des Moines 8

KANSAS:
Employment Security Division, State Labor Department, 401 Topeka Boulevard, Topeka

KENTUCKY:
Bureau of Employment Security, Department of Economic Security, Capitol Office Building, Frankfort

LOUISIANA:
Division of Employment Security, Department of Labor, P.O. Box 494, Capitol Annex Building, Baton Rouge 4

MAINE:
Employment Security Commission, 331 Water Street, Augusta

MARYLAND:
Department of Employment Security, 6 North Liberty Street, Baltimore 1

MASSACHUSETTS:
Division of Employment Security, 881 Commonwealth Avenue, Boston 15

MICHIGAN:
Employment Security Commission, 514 Boulevard Building, 7310 Woodward Avenue, Detroit 2

MINNESOTA:
Department of Employment Security, 369 Cedar Street, St. Paul 1

MISSISSIPPI:
Employment Security Commission, P.O. Box 1699, Milner Building, Jackson

MISSOURI:
Division of Employment Security, Department of Labor and Industrial Relations, 421 East Dunklin Street, Jefferson City

MONTANA:
Unemployment Compensation Commission, Sam W. Mitchell Building, P.O. Box 1728, Helena

NEBRASKA:
Division of Employment Security, Department of Labor, 134 South Twelfth Street, Lincoln 1

NEVADA:
Employment Security Department, P.O. Box 602, Carson City

NEW HAMPSHIRE:
Department of Employment Security, 34 South Main Street, Concord

NEW JERSEY:
Division of Employment Security, Department of Labor and Industry, 28 West State Street, Trenton 8

NEW MEXICO:
Employment Security Commission, 103 Sixth Street S.W., Albuquerque

NEW YORK:
Division of Employment, Department of Labor, 500 Eighth Avenue, New York 18

NORTH CAROLINA:
Employment Security Commission, P.O. Box 589, Jones and North McDowell Streets, Raleigh

NORTH DAKOTA:
North Dakota State Employment Service, 207 East Broadway, Bismarck

OHIO:
Bureau of Unemployment Compensation, 427 Cleveland Avenue, Columbus 16

OKLAHOMA:
Employment Security Commission, American National Building, Oklahoma City 2

OREGON:
Department of Employment, 513 Public Service Building, Salem

PENNSYLVANIA:
Bureau of Employment Security, Department of Labor and Industry, Seventh and Forster Streets, Harrisburg

PUERTO RICO:
Bureau of Employment Security, Department of Labor, Stop 17½ Fernandez Juncos Avenue, Santurce

RHODE ISLAND:
Department of Employment Security, 24 Mason Street, Providence 3

SOUTH CAROLINA:
Employment Security Commission, 1225 Laurel Street, Columbia 1

SOUTH DAKOTA:
Employment Security Department, 310 Lincoln Street South, Aberdeen

TENNESSEE:
Department of Employment Security, Cordell Hull State Office Building, Nashville 3

TEXAS:
Texas Employment Commission, TEC Building, Austin 1

UTAH:
Department of Employment Security, Industrial Commission, 174 Social Hall Avenue, Salt Lake City 10

VERMONT:
Unemployment Compensation Commission, 7 School Street, Montpelier

VIRGINIA:
Unemployment Compensation Commission, Broad-Grace Arcade, Richmond 11

VIRGIN ISLANDS:
Virgin Islands Employment Service, Charlotte Amalie, St. Thomas

WASHINGTON:
Employment Security Department, P.O. Box 367, Old Capitol Building, Olympia

WEST VIRGINIA:
  Department of Employment Security, State Office Building, California and Washington Streets, Charleston 5

WISCONSIN:
  Wisconsin State Employment Service, Industrial Commission, 105 South Blair Street, Madison 3

WYOMING:
  Employment Security Commission, 136½ South Wolcott Street, Casper

General Community Resources

It is not always possible for a disabled college student to receive service from a specialized agency for the physically disabled nor is it always desirable. Although this type of agency has much to offer in terms of specialized facilities, personnel, and emphasis, the general agency has its advantages. In the first place, not all services to the physically handicapped student need to be administered through specialized agencies, for example, casework and counseling. Since the dynamics of human behavior are the same for all, the case worker or counselor in a general community agency can perform invaluable service despite the absence of special training or experience in the area of physical disability. At times, the professional worker in such an agency may require consultative assistance from specialists. However, there seems to be a special value in services coming from a general community agency. Fundamentally, the disabled person is responsible to the whole community and it, in turn, is resposible to him. And also, when the disabled person receives general services it gives him a sense of being a part of the larger community.

Increasingly, general community agencies are extending educational, psychological, social, and vocational services to severely disabled persons. In the absence of a specialized resource, the college counselor may receive a certain amount of assistance from these agencies. Indeed, he is likely to find that in a proportion of cases these agencies are already participating in service to some students. For example, disabled students who are in financial need may already be known to local departments of welfare. Students with significant emotional problems may already be receiving help through a casework agency, a mental hygiene clinic, or a college counseling service. And in the medical area, many general physicians and general hospitals are interested and active in the health problems of some of the disabled students enrolled in a college or university. It may be expected that a whole host of local agencies —some of them nonspecialized in physical disability—will be participants in educational planning for disabled students. Effective college service to these students often rests on the creation and maintenance of good relationships with these other participants in the program.

NATIONAL AGENCIES

Some of the important national agencies are:

Veterans Administration, Washington 25, D.C.

Through its hospitals, regional offices, and local facilities, the Veterans Administration offers a number of comprehensive rehabilitation programs primarily designed for veterans of the United States Armed Forces. During the forties and fifties, the veteran was a familiar figure on the American campus. In those days, the Veterans Administration cooperated closely with those in charge of the administrative, personnel, and instructional work of the college. Today, even though the number of veterans attending colleges and universities is smaller, Veterans Administration personnel continue to be highly cooperative and informative.

Office of Vocational Rehabilitation, Department of Health, Education, and Welfare, Washington 25, D.C.

The Office of Vocational Rehabilitation is the national coordinating agency for the extensive State-Federal Vocational Rehabilitation Program. Much of its work is devoted to cooperative and technical activities in relation to the state agencies. More directly, however, the Office of Vocational Rehabilitation is of assistance to college and university programs through its demonstration and research grants, its publications, and its highly trained consultation staff. It sponsors important rehabilitation conferences, assists in the development of programs, and provides essential information covering a wide range of rehabilitation matters. Among its publications is *Rehabilitation Record,* a journal reflecting important developments in the field. A letter addressed to the Office of Vocational Rehabilitation will bring a number of pamphlets explaining the State-Federal Vocational Rehabilitation Program.

United States Office of Education, Department of Health, Education, and Welfare, Washington 25, D.C.

The United States Office of Education has been active in the development of special education throughout the country. Its publications have been widely used by workers in the field. It has promoted the education of exceptional individuals through supporting research projects, offering consultative services, and informing professional persons about the field. Although little emphasis has been placed on physically handicapped college students, the prospects are that an increasing interest will be taken in this group.

National Society for Crippled Children and Adults, 2023 West Ogden Avenue, Chicago 12, Illinois

The National Society for Crippled Children and Adults functions on a service basis through state affiliates which support a variety of rehabilitation programs. On the national level, the organization functions in such areas as research, professional placement, training, consultation, and publications. College and university staffs may wish to use its library facilities which include the preparation of special bibliographies, the circulation of packets of books and pamphlets, and the publication of *Rehabilitation Literature,* one of the most useful journals in this field. The central office staff is a source of valuable consultative assistance for workers in colleges and universities.

National Health Organizations

A number of privately supported organizations function on behalf of single disabilities or groups of them. These organizations almost always provide informational services, research grants, program development services, and consultative assistance. In addition, they issue publications which can be of assistance to college-level workers interested in the particular disability area. Some of the major organizations in this group are:

ALEXANDER GRAHAM BELL ASSOCIATION FOR THE DEAF, 1537 Thirty-fifth Street, N.W., Washington 7, D. C.

AMERICAN DIABETES ASSOCIATION, INC., 1 East 45th Street, New York 17, New York

AMERICAN FOUNDATION FOR THE BLIND, 15 West 16th Street, New York 11, New York

AMERICAN HEARING SOCIETY, 817 Fourteenth Street, N.W., Washington 5, D. C.

AMERICAN HEART ASSOCIATION, 44 East 23rd Street, New York 10, New York

ARTHRITIS AND RHEUMATISM FOUNDATION, 23 West 45th Street, New York 36, New York

COMMISSION ON CHRONIC ILLNESS, 615 North Wolfe Street, Baltimore 5, Maryland

MUSCULAR DYSTROPHY ASSOCIATION OF AMERICA, 39 Broadway, New York 6, New York

NATIONAL EPILEPSY LEAGUE, 130 North Wells Street, Chicago 6, Illinois

NATIONAL FOUNDATION, 120 Broadway, New York 5, New York

NATIONAL MULTIPLE SCLEROSIS SOCIETY, 270 Park Avenue, New York 17, New York

NATIONAL TUBERCULOSIS ASSOCIATION, INC., 1790 Broadway, New York 19, New York

SHUT-IN SOCIETY, INC., 221 Lexington Avenue, New York 16, New York

UNITED CEREBRAL PALSY ASSOCIATION, INC., 321 West 44th Street, New York 18, New York

Additional organizations of this type are listed in the Directory of Federal and Private Agencies working with or for the handicapped, published by the Committee for the Handicapped, Room 205, 726 Jackson Place, Washington, D. C.

PROFESSIONAL ORGANIZATIONS

A number of professional organizations have indicated special interest in disabled persons. These organizations provide a forum for persons in one or more professions, offering conferences and meetings, professional literature, and certain types of research activities.

AMERICAN ASSOCIATION FOR HEALTH, PHYSICAL EDUCATION, AND REC-
REATION (A Division of the National Education Association), 1201
Sixteenth Street, N.W., Washington 6, D. C.

AMERICAN DIETETIC ASSOCIATION, 620 North Michigan Avenue, Chicago 11, Illinois

AMERICAN HOSPITAL ASSOCIATION, 18 East Division Street, Chicago
10, Illinois

AMERICAN MEDICAL ASSOCIATION, 535 North Dearborn Street, Chicago 10, Illinois

AMERICAN NURSES ASSOCIATION, 10 Columbus Circle, New York 19,
New York

AMERICAN OCCUPATIONAL THERAPY ASSOCIATION, 33 West 42nd Street,
New York 36, New York

AMERICAN PERSONNEL AND GUIDANCE ASSOCIATION, 1534 "O" Street,
N.W., Washington 5, D. C.

AMERICAN PHYSICAL THERAPY ASSOCIATION, 1790 Broadway, New
York 19, New York

AMERICAN PSYCHOLOGICAL ASSOCIATION, 1333 Sixteenth Street, N.W.,
Washington 6, D. C.

AMERICAN PUBLIC HEALTH ASSOCIATION, 1790 Broadway, New York
19, New York

AMERICAN SPEECH AND HEARING ASSOCIATION, Wayne University, Detroit, Michigan

COUNCIL FOR EXCEPTIONAL CHILDREN (A Division of the National Education Association), 1201 Sixteenth Street, N.W., Washington 6,
D. C.

NATIONAL ASSOCIATION OF SOCIAL WORKERS, 1 Park Avenue, New
York 16, New York

NATIONAL HEALTH COUNCIL, INC., 1790 Broadway, New York 19,
New York

NATIONAL LEAGUE FOR NURSING, INC., 10 Columbus Circle, New York
19, New York

NATIONAL RECREATION ASSOCIATION, INC., 315 Fourth Avenue, New
York 10, New York

NATIONAL REHABILITATION ASSOCIATION, 1025 Vermont Avenue,
N.W., Washington 5, D. C.

PROFESSIONAL JOURNALS

Service to the physically handicapped has a relatively rich
literature. Periodicals on various phases of special education and

rehabilitation are plentiful. The list below is a partial one, suggesting some of the major publications in the field.

American Annals of the Deaf, Gallaudet College, Washington 2, D. C.

American Journal of Occupational Therapy, 33 West 42nd Street, New York 36, New York

American Journal of Physical Medicine, Mt. Royal and Guilford Avenues, Baltimore 2, Maryland

American Journal of Public Health, 1790 Broadway, New York 19, New York

Archives of Physical Medicine and Rehabilitation, 30 North Michigan Avenue, Chicago 2, Illinois

Cerebral Palsy Review, 2400 Jardine Drive, Wichita 14, Kansas

Employment Security Review, U. S. Department of Labor, Washington 25, D. C.

Exceptional Children, 1201 Sixteenth Street, N.W., Washington 6, D. C.

Journal of Chronic Diseases, C. V. Mosby Company, 3207 Washington Boulevard, St. Louis 3, Missouri

Journal of Rehabilitation, 1025 Vermont Street, N.W., Washington 5, D. C.

Journal of Speech and Hearing Disorders, University of Illinois, Urbana, Illinois

Journal of the American Medical Association, 535 North Dearborn Street, Chicago 10, Illinois

The New Outlook for the Blind, 15 West 16th Street, New York 11, New York

Personnel and Guidance Journal, 1534 "O" Street, N.W., Washington 5, D. C.

Physical Therapy Review, 1790 Broadway, New York 19, New York

Recreation, 8 West 8th Street, New York 3, New York

Rehabilitation Literature, National Society for Crippled Children and Adults, 2023 Odgen Avenue, Chicago 12, Illinois

Rehabilitation Record, Office of Vocational Rehabilitation, Department of Health, Education, and Welfare, Washington 25, D. C.

Sight-Saving Review, 1790 Broadway, New York 19, New York

Vocational Guidance Quarterly, 1534 "O" Street, N.W., Washington 5, D. C.

Volta Review, 1537 Thirty-fifth Street, N.W., Washington 7, D. C.

REFERENCE SOURCES

As mentioned earlier, the Library of the National Society for Crippled Children and Adults (2023 West Ogden Avenue, Chicago, Illinois) is an invaluable source of reference for workers interested in the physically disabled. Other professional organizations maintain library services which are helpful in compiling bibliographies and obtaining references. For example, the American Foundation for the Blind (15 West 16th Street, New York 11, New York) maintains an extensive collection of materials dealing with visual handicaps. In addition, the Institute for the Crippled and Disabled (400 First Avenue, New York 9, New York) maintains a library on rehabilitation and other phases of service to the handicapped which offers extensive resources for the professional worker.

There are a number of directories which may be helpful to persons interested in the field:

Special Education of the Exceptional, by M. Frampton and E. Gall, Volume I (Boston: Porter Sargent, 1955), contains bibliographies, lists of agencies, and suggested periodicals.

American Annals of the Deaf, January issue, contains a directory of sources of assistance for deaf persons.

The United States Department of Labor issues "State and Local Employment Security Offices."

Porter Sargent, in Boston, issues a *Directory for Exceptional Children; Schools, Services, and Other Facilities.*

The American Foundation for the Blind issues a *Directory of Activities for the Blind in the United States and Canada.*

Other lists of organizations, facilities, and resources may be obtained through the various national public and private organizations listed earlier.

Three important bibliographies are available for workers in the field of service to the disabled:

R. G. Barker and others, *Adjustment to Physical Handicap and Illness* (New York: Social Science Research Council, 1956).

Earl C. Graham and Marjorie M. Mullen, *Rehabilitation Literature 1950–55* (New York: McGraw-Hill Book Co., Inc., 1956).

Maya Riviere, *Rehabilitation of the Handicapped: A Bibliography, 1940–46* (New York: National Council on Rehabilitation, 1949).

These bibliographies cover specific periods in the literature. However, they are brought up to date by various periodicals in the field which carry current references and annotations. Among these are:

The American Personnel and Guidance Journal
Exceptional Children
The New Outlook for the Blind
Psychological Abstracts
Rehabilitation Literature
Sociological Abstracts

As indicated earlier, the volume of writing in all areas of physical disability is extensive, and relatively complete bibliographies are available. While numerous worth-while items are available, the books on special education and rehabilitation listed below constitute a beginning:

ALLAN, W. SCOTT, *Rehabilitation: A Community Challenge* (New York: John Wiley & Sons, Inc., 1958).

BAKER, HARRY J., *Introduction to Exceptional Children,* Third Edition (New York: The Macmillan Company, Inc., 1959).

BARKER, R. G., AND OTHERS, *Adjustment to Physical Handicap and Illness* (New York: Social Science Research Council, 1956).

CRUICKSHANK, WILLIAM M., AND OTHERS, *Education of Exceptional Children and Youth* (Englewood Cliffs, N. J.: Prentice-Hall, Inc., 1958).

CRUICKSHANK, WILLIAM M., AND OTHERS, *Psychology of Exceptional Children and Youth* (Englewood Cliffs, N. J.: Prentice-Hall, Inc., 1955).

CRUICKSHANK, W. M., AND RAUS, G. M., EDITORS, *Cerebral Palsy* (Syracuse, N. Y.: Syracuse University Press, 1955).

GOWMAN, A. G., *The War-Blind in American Social Structure* (New York: American Foundation for the Blind, 1957).

HATHAWAY, W., AND OTHERS, *Education and Health of the Partially Seeing Child,* Fourth Edition (New York: Columbia University Press, 1959).

KESSLER, HENRY H., *Rehabilitation of the Physically Handicapped,* Revised Edition (New York: Columbia University Press, 1953).

LEVINE, E. S., *Youth in a Soundless World* (New York: New York University Press, 1956).

LOFQUIST, LLOYD H., *Vocational Counseling with the Physically Handicapped* (New York: Appleton-Century-Crofts, Inc., 1957).

LOUTTIT, C. M., *Clinical Psychology of Exceptional Children,* Third Edition (New York: Harper & Brothers, 1957).

PATTISON, HARRY A., *The Handicapped and Their Rehabilitation* (Springfield, Ill.: Charles C Thomas, 1957).

UNITED STATES DEPARTMENT OF HEALTH, EDUCATION, AND WELFARE, *Workshops for the Disabled* (Washington, D. C.: Government Printing Office, 1956).

WEST, R., AND OTHERS, *The Rehabilitation of Speech* (New York: Harper & Brothers, 1957).